U R The Solution

An AO Adventure

By Mark Victor Hansen and Bill Froehlich

PUBLISHED BY FASTPENCIL, INC.

YOU ARE INVITED TO
THE RED CARPET WORLD TOUR PREMIER
OF
U R THE SOLUTION
ON
THE
BIG SCREEN
Go
To
www.urthesolutionthebook.com

Allow us to open the portal to your imagination
and step into a playful new reality and discover that
U R
The
Solution!
❧

"U R the Solution is the Harry Potter meets Lord of the Rings of the next generation. Get ready for a whirlwind story and a massive, major motion picture."
Austin Walsh, Social Media Phenomenon

"Mark Victor and Bill will take you on an exciting Spiritual trip so far outside of the box that your perception of your life will change forever. You will begin thinking on a much higher frequency and your life will be what you have been dreaming of for years."
—Bob Proctor, Best-selling author, Born Rich, Speaker, as seen on The Secret

"Out of the greatest crises come the greatest innovations. This decade should see the greatest entrepreneurial revolution ever. This book invites you to join— by simply and brilliantly showing you how to expand your awareness to focus on the solution, not the problem."
Harry S. Dent, Jr., author of The Great Depression Ahead

"Have you ever had the feeling you need to be taken by the hand and guided to a better place? In U R the Solution, the lovable AO takes you on a liberating adventure, revealing the magic that really IS waiting to happen in your life right now… and showing you just how to make it happen. If you're ready to break out and experience the adventure of true success, grab this book and a chair and start your first AO journey as fast as you can!"
—Crystal Dwyer, author and International Speaker, Pure Thoughts for Pure Results & Living the Skinny Life-The Real Skinny on Fit, Slim, & Healthy

"U R the Solution illuminates the infinite possibilities that the universe offers to all. True to its title, U R the Solution cleverly illustrates the true potential in each of us to create a personal solution as well as a global solution to the many challenges facing each of us. U R the Solution is a timely and much needed brilliantly written book! Be sure to share this book with your friends, business associates, and particularly with your loved ones, including your children!"
–Harry Singer, Speaker, Entrepreneur, President of Ultra International

"This wonderful, warm, inspiring book will trigger your imagination and wake you to the unlimited potential that lies within you right now, teaching you how to activate your possibilities and achieve all your goals."
–Brian Tracy, Best-selling author and Professional Speaker

"Prepare to awaken your full economic potential! Read this book!"
–Sharon Lechter, co-author, Rich Dad, Poor Dad

॰

CONTENTS

DEDICATION

Thank you for being excited to share AO with the wonderful world of happy readers. I deeply appreciate your understanding of what it takes to make it happen, effectively and totally. U R my sol ution to a lively life magnificently, completely and fully lived. U R the most exquisitely exciting and together woman in the world, my beloved Crystal.

    –Mark Victor Hansen

To my beloved parents, William R. B. and Mina G. Froehlich, who proved with their lives that Love is the foundation we all stand upon. They have my eternal gratitude for showing me the way to live by being Love-in-action. And to my wonderful sister, Marcy Froehlich, an artistically talented and successful costume designer who is the complete expression of grace and kindness. I am in awe of your expressed qualities.

    –Bill Froehlich

Nothing happens until something moves.
~Albert Einstein

PREFACE TO THE PREFACE

We are talking here about starting before the beginning. True, no other book starts here, but then this is an original, unlike anything you have ever read. We predict it will unequivocally be the most enlightening, thought provoking, mind challenging, and talked-about book that you have ever read, discussed, ingested and digested. It will wow your soul and make your pocketbook grow. Drink deeply of its wisdom, allow your awareness to expand; then, read it as a fable that will enable ...

Why? Our preposterous offer is because if you are aligned with your divine source **ANYTHING IS POSSIBLE**. In fact, **EVERY-THING IS POSSIBLE**. Each and every one of us has a clear path. **You matter! You are vital!** If you are not thinking clearly, it is easy to *feel* and *be* lost. This book is a clear guide on how to get on the path—and stay on it.

We start at the end, with a private conversation between you and our main character—who is a real character—AO. In case you are wondering, that's pronounced A-Oh. That will prevent your tongue getting all twisted and tangled learning to pronounce his real name, which you will discover later ... if you read on.

AO has profoundly important ideas to share with your soul, so get ready ...

Dear Reader,

When is the last time you had a *good soul talking-to*? Sure, you have had heart-to-hearts and head-to-heads, but I want to talk to you soul to soul … core essence to core essence. You are … you *are* a soul. You don't *have* a soul. A soul is your source energy—inside outing.

You think that you take your soul to church, temple, or your place of worship and you are done after a few hours of retreating there. Well, your soul is desperate for more communication. Read this unfolding and ongoing story. It will make your heart sing, because it is the story of every man and every woman. It is your unfolding and expanding story. Prepare to be enlightened.

Your soul is your awareness. Your soul is the truth of you. Your soul is a broadcasting and receiving station for all that you have done, are doing, and will ever do. You have your hand on the tuning dial. *If you know how, you can tune in to infinite possibilities.* I, AO, will tell you how, so listen closely, my friend.

The Universe conspires to serve and bless you, absolutely and totally, every day! It conspires to make you prosperous, if you have the right purpose in your soul. Everything is working together for your good. Success is your natural and normal condition. *If you don't have it, it is because you are hindering it.* Like the sandbags on a hot air balloon, you may be hindering its natural progress with sandbags of fear, greed, anxiety, guilt, anger, ambition, and any self-sabotaging behavior. Loose them, and let them go.

Abundance—financial or otherwise—has nothing to do with your education or lack of education or a business plan or lack of one. It is a state of mind, one your soul knows infinitely well. It is a spiritual experience. The whisper in your heart says: *U were put here to succeed. That is your natural state and U just have to recognize and accept it now.*

U R your awareness, out-pictured. Your awareness creates all that can ever be or become. There is no shortage of food, water, energy, clothing or anything else. That statement is made knowing full well the challenges that exist on this planet, the perceived problems. Your awareness can create abundance of all things, everywhere. Always. If U R aware enough.

When U R in perfect peace with your natural state, U R like a drop of rain that falls in a stream and blends with the surrounding water and naturally goes with the flow. You are at one with all that surrounds you. You are here to re-create the Garden of Eden with abundance and plenty for you and yours and more than enough—yes—absolute plentitude for everyone, everywhere on Spaceship Earth.

This is awareness. *It's the beginning of your beginning*. Most people think of it as an ending, a place you have to get to, somewhere over there. They fear that the road there is long and hard and takes time. In your heart, U already know that it is here, now, and is the place you come from. U were born complete with an inner GPS, your emotional guidance system.

The dawning of this new awareness will cause a *shift in consciousness* that will travel around the world as the positive and exciting winds of change.

And U—yes, U!—R the creator of your experience, your life, and U will take this fable, like the one about the 'Emperor having no clothes,' and metaphorically re-dress the world by thinking new thoughts, dreaming impossible dreams, and boldly venturing forth.

You can and will and must freely imagine possibilities, those wonderful discoveries that are imagined by the one before they can be used by the many. Jules Verne, the great science fiction author, wrote in the 1860s that humans would fly above the ground, dive deep into the sea, burrow into the Earth, and rocket into space. The Wright brothers believed Verne, created a theory from his fiction, and flew fourteen feet at Kitty Hawk—launching the innovative world of aviation. Jacques Cousteau believed Verne and invented Aqualungs and created scuba diving in the Sixties. Scientists and geologists use laser beams to cut into Mother Earth with effortless ease; Werner Von Braun believed we could land a man on the moon and got President John F. Kennedy to deliver the goods. U R here to do the same and more and more ...

You now have my absolute and complete permission. I'm expecting greatness from you and there is much love for you here. Fully expect that this day will bring you a blessing, as will every day from now on.

If you find that hard to believe, then you really, truly, absolutely *must* read on; only *be warned* that what you discover may make you deliriously happy and successful and vitally alive!

Affectionately Yours,

AO

PREFACE

U R, beloved reader, the trim tab on society's great ship of state. A trim tab is like a miniature rudder attached to the big rudder of a ship or airplane. Turning the trim tab builds a low pressure that pulls the big rudder around. It takes very little effort. One little trim tab—one person—and the ship of state turns in a new direction.

Tough barnacles cling stubbornly to the side of ocean-going vessels. Barnacles are crustaceans which glue themselves to the bottom of a ship. Like entrenched thoughts and beliefs, they are extremely difficult to dislodge, unless the vessel sails into *fresh water* ... and then they fall off effortlessly.

We invite U to allow these magical, mystical pages to become the fresh water that dislodges the long-held beliefs that limit our lives, communities, states, nations and world. Set sail with us, barnacle-free, with your hand on the trim tab, to explore the wonders of our universe and have a life-changing ... ***AO Adventure.***

CHAPTER ONE
Temperature Rising

1

TEMPERATURE RISING

In their original innocence, they heard the clouds talk to them. They were willing to hear and believe because they hadn't been educated *not* to believe in their dreams and visions.

Lying on their backs on a summer day with the grass tickling their feet, they heard the talking clouds. In that divine moment of not doubting, everything began ...

Ashley and Brian were the very best of friends. Childlike at heart and infinitely curious, their creativity was playful and they trusted their connection to the wonderful world around them. But this was no ordinary day. Change was in the air.

Though immersed in their innocence, they were not naïve; they were aware of their world's problems, had heard it from their parents, friends, newspapers, magazines, TV and the web. They felt it in the air and saw it etched on people's faces. Yet their innocence anchored them in hope.

Ashley stared up at the rolling white clouds with almost delirious delight. Her thoughts came as gentle whispers in her head, soft as mist, like a tickle from your heart. Unable to resist her enchanting thought, a smile scrambled across her lips. "I just had a vision that we can save the world," uttered Ashley joyously and breathlessly.

"How?" inquired Brian, enticed by the joy he saw on Ashley's face.

"I don't know ... It's crazy, isn't it?" Ashley stared up at the clouds in wonder.

"Why not?" said Brian, hope rising like an unstoppable tide inside him. "What if we could? That'd be cool."

Their thoughts danced with delight at the possibility of it all. They watched spellbound as the white clouds above them undulated with the same rapturous rhythm as the thoughts that were sculpting their dreams. Their dreams soared and set sail for lands of magical, unlimited possibilities, and light sparkled in their eyes from the visions.

As their arms stretched out over the cool ground, bending blades of grass, their fingers felt the wet dew and the sensuous touch brought their thoughts down from the clouds.

"Do you know how? How we save the world?" wondered Ashley.

"Sure ... well ... " Brian wasn't all that sure. "I guess they might think ... "

"That we don't count," said Ashley, "because we're ... just us."

"Yeah," agreed Brian. "We're just kids."

An ominous black cloud hovering heavily above them said, "Almost everyone desperately believes in end times ... and that's a point of view you've heard your parents discuss."

A billowy white cloud wiggled her silky self right above the dark mass and said, "All he says may be; yet from up here, I can see possibilities for a new and better tomorrow."

Ashley and Brian were different than their parents, for not once did they think *I find that hard to believe.* Nor did they say *It's impos-*

sible. I can't hear a cloud think, talk, give advice, or see it wiggle, all of which happened on that fateful day.

Sunlight burst through the smiling mouth of the white cloud as she said knowingly, "As I taught Einstein, nothing happens until something moves. You see, momentum has to begin somewhere. Somewhere in your mind."

Thundering in dissent and with a bolt of lightning for emphasis, the dark cloud bellowed, "The problem's not in your mind, it's in your wallet! And there's not much left! That's a problem that's way bigger than you are!" While it spoke, the dark cloud moved in front of the sun and the kids were suddenly cold.

The young boy and girl looked at each other. This felt different, and not good. For the first time, they wondered how they could get away from this bad feeling. It blotted out the smiling light. It was scary and they found themselves breathing faster. "I don't want to be here, I want to be somewhere else," Brian pleaded. "How do we get somewhere else? I don't know how to do that!" exclaimed Ashley.

The white cloud laughed and a spray of sunlight whipped away the darkness. "U R where you need to be, because U R here to save the world and make a difference that makes a difference. The solutions are all around you, but you don't see them because you need to look at things differently. It's like I told Albert long ago, you can't solve the problem at the level of the problem; you gotta go *above* the problem, so you need a MacGyver-like solution. Remember that great TV character who escaped from problems using whatever was around him in infinitely inventive ways?"

Brian sighed, thinking of his father. "My Dad says that a paper-clip, a crummy gum wrapper, and some duct tape's not gonna Mac-Gyver us out of *this* economic mess."

Ashley piped in, "Yeah I heard my Mom say that our goose was cooked, and we don't even have a goose!"

"Well I guess she's never heard the people who quote me in the computer business," the white cloud laughed. "You got to get above it, go into the cloud, they say! That would be a cloud of right, creative thinking, by the way. That's where the solutions are, not at the level of the problem. And this time the problem is so big it needs everyone's right, creative thinking to get us to the solutions."

"Then you're never going to make it!" shouted the dark cloud. The heavy words fell as wet globules of darkness that landed all around Ashley and Brian as they dodged and ducked. "There is no way everyone's thinking has a place to go. You're all just wandering around in the dark bumping into each other and getting stuck!"

The roiling black cloud spat out some more gloppy goops of darkness, trapping Ashley and Brian so they couldn't move. Ashley watched wide-eyed as a glob of darkness melted the ground away ... leaving a dripping hole filled with *red ink*.

As the two kids clung to each other, the white cloud simply continued. "The solutions already have been created. You're here to discover and become aware of them. The principles of mathematics have always been available, even when we were wandering around in caves. Two times two always equals four; this cannot rust out, wear out, get tired or scared, or go on vacation. It is a concept. It is an awareness. You are here to become aware."

The girl and boy were excited. The seeds of their dream began to take form.

While they were pondering, they did not notice the dark cloud slowly descend through the trees, ever closer to them, slurping its way as a clinging mist. Its turning and twisting shape-shifted into a new and pleasing form—a new friend, just like them.

He said his name was Tommy and that he liked what they were saying. He placed cold hands on their shoulders and said, "Did you see that dark cloud hanging around here? That's a bad storm cloud and it could wash away everything." Suddenly fearful, the boy and girl looked around. Tommy added ominously, "It's going to get worse unless somebody does something about it. We better go find somebody. Somebody bigger than us. Somebody who knows better."

As they listened to him, a fog surrounded them. Now they didn't know which way to turn. They were lost. As Tommy walked ahead of them they felt alone and scared and were losing more confidence with every step.

When they followed Tommy, not wanting to be all alone and thinking their new friend had the answers, their goose bumps were popping and their internal guidance systems were shouting *Don't go with Tommy!* Yet they wondered where they would go if they didn't go with Tommy, because clearly a bad storm was brewing.

Tommy said, "Look, isn't this cool?" He pointed to a path of leaves on which every leaf seemed properly connected. "Look how everything fits so perfectly. Let's go. This path has been around for a long time. Can you see where all the footprints stepped before? Just place your feet in the same place. It's easy."

In a rush of excitement Ashley and Brian ran down the path, until the flimsy leaves unexpectedly caved in beneath their feet. They gasped helplessly … and plummeted down into the darkness.

Your problems begin when you think you are separated from your Divine Source.

CHAPTER TWO
The Collapse

2

THE COLLAPSE

Falling through darkness was like swimming through feathers or climbing an air wall—so disorienting. Ashley and Brian felt their breath leak out through their toes and their skin stretch into flubbery folds of flapping flab.

Eyes closed, frightened to the core of their beings, they reached out for each other as they fell. Just as their hands clasped, they bounced off thick, invisible globs of darkness, then fell further until landing with a painful thud.

At first they weren't at all sure that they had landed *on* anything. The falling feeling was so riveted in their thinking that they were still dizzy with motion madness.

Finally, they dared to open their eyes. Slowly they looked at each other, half expecting the other to look like a squished marshmallow. It was strange and unsettling to see that they were okay. They were certain they should be twisted like pretzels or that limbs would plop off at any second. They each did a full body scan, their eyes bulging in disbelief that they weren't broken, bruised or busted.

"I'm okay, are you okay?" blurted Brian.

"Yeah, I think I'm okay." Ashley looked at her body, perplexed. "How did we fall that far and not get broken?"

They looked at each other, not knowing what to do next.

"You stand up first," dared Ashley.

"Couldn't we just sit here until someone finds us?" Brian wasn't sure the ground they were sitting on was all that solid. "I don't wanna fall through anything else."

"Don't you wanna know where we are? I wanna know where we are." Ashley gamely peered over her shoulder. "Maybe it's not that bad."

"Yeah," sniped Brian, "that's what my mom said when my dad said everything crashed. Then he showed her their account or something and she just sat down and cried. She didn't even fix dinner that night."

Ashley wondered, "What happened, didn't she move?"

"No, just sat there, all hunched over. My dad's really bad at boiling water so I got to call up and order pizza, which was fun, until my mom started crying and wouldn't stop." Brian gazed off, hoping the memory would go away.

Ashley's own memory wasn't far from her thoughts and rose up quickly. "I know, my dad did a lot of staring, and my mom just started cleaning the house—she really hates cleaning the house—and she never asked me to do anything. It was really weird. I didn't like it. And that's why I don't wanna sit here anymore."

Upon standing, Ashley realized they should leave, and right away. "We're in a cave," she said. And indeed they were. Lying in a small crater of globby darkness, they had not known how close the walls were and that they were mere feet from the exit.

"Oh, cool." Now Brian was excited. Ashley emphatically pointed to the wall's edge at the exit. Carved in the craggy stone face were the words *Cave of Calamity*. Brian took Ashley's hand and together they stepped boldly and quickly out of the *Cave of Calamity*, not wanting to stay one minute longer in a place named *Cave of Calamity*.

To their initial delight and surprise, they discovered they were in a misty, moist environment that felt like Ireland in spring. Leaves were dripping as they walked wide-eyed in this new environment. When they looked back, they could not see where they had come from; they did not know where they were, and for sure they did not know where they were going. Even the entrance of the *Cave of Calamity* was nowhere to be seen.

Ashley and Brian looked around for Tommy, but they were alone. Absolutely alone. Behind them, they suddenly heard a voice, *"Remember, you always have a choice in how you look at things."*

They spun around to the voice and saw no one but a little squirrel with white fur and pink eyes, covered in silky strips of glowing white mist and staring at them intently. Ashley looked at Brian and asked, "Who said that?" Brian had no idea. They both looked at the squirrel, who stared right back at them then rubbed his little paws together, showering the ground in front of him with wisps of white mist.

The two kids turned away from the squirrel, looking for the voice, thinking now that it might have been an echo from a distance. They did not see the squirrel scramble off the rock on which he was perched, and they certainly did not see the squirrel as it swirled into a white mist and drifted upward on the breeze.

Brian, confused and more than a little frightened, managed to whisper, "Maybe nobody said anything, 'cause we're alone ... aren't we?" Ashley grabbed hold of his hand. Neither noticed the white mist that drifted around behind them and settled to the ground.

When the mist struck the earth, it thickened and rose, forming a foot, then a leg covered in flowing alabaster robes that encased a body that filled out, until on top of it all a head with long, thick, tousled blond hair took shape above the collar. The figure had an

aura of energy spreading before him and a resonant voice that surrounded them in vibrations. *"We are never really alone, are we … if
we listen?"*

Ashley and Brian spun around to catch the last of his words.
They heard him but his lips had not moved. His words echoed res-
onantly in their minds. He spoke without talking. To each of them
it seemed impossible and they were completely flabbergasted.
Their mouths dropped open and stayed open.

"That's a great way to catch bugs. I like doing that a lot." Now
his lips moved and he smiled, giving them a feeling of instantaneous comfort as his words again echoed inside them. ***"Fear not,
little ones, for that's where we start."***

"Start what?" stuttered Brian.

"Start the rest of everything, of course," he smiled. "Your fear
has no power unless you give it power. You give it all the power it
will ever have."

"Don't you have a name?" asked Brian. "Or do you just say
smart sounding stuff to kids?"

Ashley's words tumbled out of her mouth. "Why did you bring
us here, where are we, and who are you?"

"I'll answer in reverse," he smiled. "I am that I am. And you are
where you are. You are where you need to be. I brought you here
because you are critical to the future of the planet."

Brian and Ashley blurted together, "Us?!"

"U R," he nodded. "You asked if you could save the planet and
make a difference, didn't you?"

"Um, ah, yes I did," said Ashley, astonished. "You heard that?"

"Un huh," he responded.

"Are you sure we're the ones? Why us?" Ashley and Brian were
perplexed.

As he spoke, fluttery wisps of mist floated from his mouth like
warm breath on a cold day. ***"I've been here before fear, and I'll
be here after.*** That's how I know who you are. And that's enough

for now," and he laughed, spewing puffballs of white mist that bounced off their heads. "What's more important is that we be introduced," he grinned deliciously. "My name is Mr. Agemodnaahpla. But you can call me AO. That's short for when you read it backwards."

"Mr. what?" Brian was suddenly distracted by a mist ball as it bounced onto his head and rolled down onto his nose and hung there, suspended. He tried to push it off his nose with his finger but it stuck to his finger, and no matter how hard he shook it, the puffy mist ball stayed put.

"Mr. Agemodnaahpla," he said, "Go ahead, try it backwards."

Ashley squinted in concentration and slowly said, "Mr. Alp . . haa . . n . . do . . me . . ga. Is that right?"

"No, but that was fun." He was clearly enjoying this, in a playful way.

Brian took a deep breath to blow the mist ball from his finger but instead sucked it right into his mouth. He gasped, horrified. "I swallowed it!"

"Yum," was all Mr. Agemodnaahpla said.

Ashley was not giving up. "Well then it's got to be ... Al . . pha . . and . . o . . mega. Alpha and Omega?"

"That's it, bravo, quite right," said Mr. Agemodnaahpla.

"But that's three names," ventured Brian, now that he realized he wasn't poisoned by the mist ball.

"No, one name, Alpha and Omega, AO for short." AO looked at them and folded his arms across his chest as his alabaster robes billowed toward them. "So, now what?"

"Are you going to help us?" Brian looked at AO hopefully.

"Always!" AO said. "What do you want?"

"We're lost and we wanna go home," Brian responded.

"You see yourself as lost?" AO raised an eyebrow in anticipation of their answer.

"Well ... yeah ... 'cause we are lost," said Ashley.

"So," he said, folding his arms again. His alabaster robe billowed outward and showered them in mist sparkles. "You think and see and feel and believe that you're lost."

Both kids nodded in agreement.

"Is that what home looks like?"

Both kids shook their heads. Then AO stretched out his arms and opened his palms. In each hand was a laser-like light sculpture of Ashley and Brian's homes. "Is this what your homes look like?" Both kids vigorously nodded in agreement. AO slowly closed his hands, making the homes disappear.

AO quickly reached down and grabbed the ground. He pulled upward and stretched out a rectangular block of clay like an accordion, then let go and the block stood up on its own. He reached into his robe, withdrew two sculptor's chisels and handed them to the kids.

"Go ahead and carve an elephant from this block of clay," he said to both of them, "but do it while you look at this." He pointed at the gnarly, twisted trunk of an oak tree.

They chiseled energetically, hoping to sculpt an elephant. But their eyes looked only upon the gnarled oak tree, so no matter how much they chiseled and chopped, their sculpture stubbornly resembled a gnarly, twisted trunk of an oak tree and not an elephant.

AO watched their frustration grow and waited until their hopes faded before he spoke. "In your life, you will carve whatever you look at, whatever you think about, and whatever you feel and believe. You are the sculptor of your entire life and your future destiny."

"But how do we see our way home when we don't know where we are or how we got here?" Brian looked at AO forlornly as Ashley nodded in depressed agreement.

"You gotta start at the end, not the beginning, to get where you want to go. Because if you don't know where you want to go, any road will take you. And that, my dear friends, is where most people are and why you see yourselves and your world in so much trouble. Your beliefs keep you anchored in the problem."

He certainly had their attention. Ashley and Brian were well aware of the problems that everyone talked about. They had heard their parents talking about it, and their friends and teachers at school, and when flipping around on the TV they just kept seeing the problem. Nearly everyone talked about it, and it wasn't fun talk either. There were not a lot of laughs. People were scared but they tried hard not to show it.

AO knew their thoughts even before they did, but he let the doubts register on their young faces until he knew they might be ready to hear what he had to say. "You've been playing the game, haven't you? You and your parents and your friends."

The two kids didn't know what game he was talking about. Brian offered a half-hearted admittance as he said, "Well, we played Scrabble last night." Ashley quickly piped in with, "And I won at Monopoly—I wiped everyone out." She looked at AO with hopeful eyes. "Does that count? Do we get to go home now?"

"Those are fun games," said AO. "Did you know that q-o-p-h and q-a-t are usable words? You can score a lot of points with those. What fun! Especially when no one believes you. And owning the railroads is a little secret. My friend Warren Buffett really did that with Burlington Northern. He's good at playing those games because it's all a joy to him, doing what he loves." AO paused, savoring the delight of the moment, then remembered where he was. "Ahh, but I was thinking of something else, another game. Wanna guess?"

Both kids quickly shook their heads.

AO shrugged and continued. *"Fear invites you to play, for it can't play alone.* Alone, it has nowhere to go and nothing to do. So it simply must have its way to stay. It's learned to be subtle or loud and especially convincing to get you to play. And most of all, it never wants the game to end."

"But we still don't know how to get home!" blurted Ashley.

"Because you fear the problem's too big," responded AO. "You think it's too complicated and you feel trapped. You may have to think differently about that."

Brian moaned, "But there are no signs around here and we don't have a map."

"But this ... but that ... but this ... but that ... hmmm," mused AO. "Okay, try this. I want you to walk forward down that path, but you must look at your butts at all times."

Ashley and Brian were eager to get home, so they followed AO's instructions. They stepped forward down the path in front of them, yet as soon as they looked behind them at their butts they began to wobble and weave in circles like they were chasing their tails. They went nowhere but round and round until they tripped over their own feet and tumbled to the ground in a hopeless heap.

"We didn't get anywhere! That was a dumb direction," complained Ashley.

"Exactly," said AO. "When looking at your 'buts' you can't see where you're going. That's why your butt's behind you—and that's where you should leave all your other 'buts,' if you want to go home."

"Couldn't you just give us a map?" asked Brian, a little annoyed.

"Here is your map," said AO. "It's always been with you." He looked directly into their eyes. "If you want to experience something in this life, you must become what it is you wish to live. You will move faster when you don't move *toward* something, but know and feel that you are already *there*."

Ashley wondered, "Is this some kind of magic?"

"What is, is," stated AO simply. "It's how you look at it."

Both kids tried to grasp what he was saying. AO smiled benignly, giving no other clues. When Brian looked around, doubts grew within his thoughts. "I guess we're in trouble . . ." he looked out over the green valley, flourishing with abundant life. "because I can't see my house from here." Ashley chimed in as she took his hand, "And neither can I."

When the two kids turned back to where AO stood, all that was left was a silky, white mist that touched everything, everywhere. Its presence didn't distort the view of anything on which it rested. The purity of its white color held all colors, yet the truth of what lay beneath its misty breath was clearly seen.

Ashley cried out. "Where did you go, AO?" Silence was the only response. Brian clung tighter to her hand. "Now we're really in trouble."

In response to their fear of being alone, the sky above them seemed to fill with dark and looming clouds, obscuring the bright sunlight that was still shining.

"Which way do you think we go?" wondered Brian.

"I don't know," said Ashley. "It all looks the same."

As their fear increased, the dark clouds swirled lower and lower until one of them touched the ground. It was darkness piled higher, one glob on top of another, until an ill wind blew around it, sculpting a shape that was Tommy.

Ashley and Brian excitedly turned around, hearing a rush of noise behind them. Seeing Tommy, they were delighted to no longer be alone.

"Hey kids, I've been here before and I can get us out of here," said Tommy.

"Let's go! How do we get out of here?" implored Ashley.

"We all fell down and got here together," said Tommy. "Where I want to take you, we'll have endless play and ice cream every day."

"Endless play and ice cream every day?" both chimed in, incredulous but hopeful. "Really? Can we really do that?" asked Brian. "Yeah, really?" repeated Ashley.

"Don't you want to?" asked Tommy. "'Cause if you really want to, I can make it happen." Tommy waited until they were fully captivated by this idea.

While Ashley and Brian toyed with this thought, AO watched them from the majestic mountainside, his head now as big as Mount Rushmore. His glowing countenance looked on with a bemused smile.

Brian suddenly caught a glance of AO and exclaimed, "Hey, isn't that—"

Just as the words stumbled from Brian's mouth, Tommy grabbed him and quickly turned him away from AO, then in a stern voice commanded, "If we don't go now, you'll lose everything!" Without waiting for response, he walked off across dark stepping stones, his exit threatening to leave them alone.

Gripped by a sudden rush of fear, Brian grabbed Ashley. "We'd better follow him or we'll be lost forever!"

"Now let's go down this path, but you gotta listen to me and do exactly what I say, because I've seen all the problems up ahead, and there are a lot of them," said Tommy.

"Where's AO, isn't he coming too?" asked Ashley, looking around.

"If this AO guy was a real friend, he would've taken you out of here himself." Tommy gestured, "Now look around, he's nowhere to be found."

Ashley and Brian looked around, hoping to find AO, but all they saw was the dark gray mist hanging in the air and blocking their view. They trembled with fear, doubt and foreboding. They hoped that Tommy had the answer and knew the way home.

As Tommy led them forward, he said, "Let me tell you what you're gonna see …" but his words drifted off as Ashley and Brian saw two little, white squirrels with dazzling pink eyes, rearing up on their haunches and offering two pair of glasses with crystal-clear lenses.

"Oh cute, Bri, look at these guys," cooed Ashley.

Brian leaned down to grab both glasses and handed one to Ashley. He noticed that the bow was engraved and imprinted with the words *Fear Free Glasses.*

Ashley put them on right away and was astonished. "Wow, look at this, everything's so beautiful! Let's stay here, this is paradise!"

Tommy grabbed Brian's glasses, saying, "Let me clean those for you." As he wiped the lenses of the glasses, they slowly grew darker. He handed them back to Brian. "Aren't these cool?" said Tommy. "Sunglasses!"

Meanwhile, Ashley looked all around for 360 degrees with her new glasses, completely in awe of everything she saw. Through her lenses, Tommy was nowhere to be seen. "Hey, Bri ... where's Tommy?"

Brian put on the now-darker "sunglasses" and saw Tommy right in front of him. "He's right here. What's wrong with you, can't you see him? You better let Tommy clean your glasses." With that, Brian reached over, removed Ashley's glasses and handed them to Tommy, who proceeded to quickly clean them to a darker shade.

When Ashley put on the newly "cleaned" glasses, she was sorely disappointed. "Where did paradise go?"

"That's where I'm taking you, it's up ahead!" exclaimed Tommy.

"Let's go, I haven't seen it yet and I want to," piped in Brian

The two albino squirrels bounded along behind them, merging into one squirrel as they scrambled up the bark of a tree trunk, then leaping from branch to branch, chasing after the trio until coming to rest on the longest branch just before them on the path.

Brian caught the squirrel out of the corner of his eye and witnessed it morph into a great white owl, which winked at him. *"Place the glasses in the pocket over your heart. You'll know why later."* As they traipsed along behind Tommy, Ashley placed her glasses in her shirt pocket over her heart. Brian saw this and wondered if she had heard the same echo in her mind as he had. He, too, slipped the glasses into the pocket over his heart.

The great white owl didn't look worried as Ashley and Brian walked away from him. He knew a secret they would discover: to understand more deeply, they had to play with fear for awhile. But his words were written deeply and unforgettably in their hearts as a vibration of love.

As they walked through the lush green fields and stepped across a babbling brook on slippery stones, Tommy went on and on about the problems they would face. The more he spoke, the more concerned Ashley and Brian became, and the more worried they were about the looming problems ahead. The kids struggled over the slippery stones while Tommy skipped and danced across the rocks as sure-footed as a mountain goat.

Tommy spoke eloquently of the problems that the kids had heard from their parents and the media. He spoke with passion about foreclosures, bankruptcy, unaffordable health care, crumbling education, immigration gone wild, depleted energy, scarcity of water, exploding population, calamitous climate changes, manmade environmental disasters like oozing oil in the Gulf of Mexico, and on and on and on …

Tommy's words sprayed ahead of him, tumbling from his mouth as loose letters that fell like seeds to the ground. Soon they sprang up from the soil as little sprigs, then trunks with tiny leafy twigs, then trees that rose up like launched rockets whose intertwined branches blotted out the sun.

Ashley and Brian struggled to keep up, nervously glancing around with a feeling of trepidation at the strange occurrences that seemed out of their control. They looked only to Tommy for guidance. Their own instincts were no longer trusted. Forgotten was the sensation from their inner compass. They were now deep into the Forest of Fear, with no end in sight.

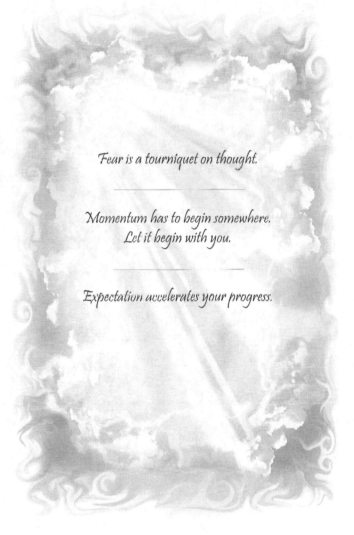

Fear is a tourniquet on thought.

Momentum has to begin somewhere.
Let it begin with you.

Expectation accelerates your progress.

CHAPTER THREE
Clouds of Choice

3

CLOUDS OF CHOICE

Branches slapped at their arms and legs, constantly and painfully reminding them of the fears surrounding them on all sides. With the wind howling and the shadows creepily crawling around them, they didn't know what to expect next. Tommy marched them deeper and deeper into the foreboding darkness of the forest. Their fears loomed as high as the tallest tree and they had goose bumps on their goose bumps.

"What do we do now? I'm scared to death!" Ashley exclaimed under her breath to Brian as she tugged at his shirttail. "This is worse than my worst nightmare."

Brian was not exactly a bastion of bravado and machismo either. "Tommy said he knew how to get us out of here. I guess we gotta listen to him now," Brian said as he looked around, hoping to find an exit. "I don't know where we are or where we've been or where we're going."

Tommy turned around, walking backwards, and addressed Ashley and Brian. "Be careful where you walk, because you're walking on your future energy."

Brian looked down, "What?!" he exclaimed. He tried to sidestep something that he didn't even know was there and managed to fall over his own feet and tumble to the ground.

Ashley burst out laughing until Tommy pointed at the ground and told her to be careful, and she too tripped over her own feet trying to avoid something she couldn't even see.

"What energy am I stepping on?" asked Brian, as he scrambled back up on his feet. "I don't see any energy."

Tommy knelt down and brushed aside some fallen leaves and loose soil, uncovering the tiny bones of a small animal. "Like the dinosaurs, these bones will be preserved deep in the soil, and along with other compressed elements will one day come back as oil. We need all the oil we can find to run this world. Without oil, we all collapse. We use it in just about everything."

As Tommy swept aside more dirt with his fingers, Ashley and Brian's mouths dropped open. They found themselves staring at a holographic pictorial view that seemed to extend deep into the earth. It showed the process of oil being formed over one hundred and sixty million years, in a time-elapsed progression that created the hydrocarbons.

"Look how long it took to make this," Tommy said solemnly. "Surely, something that takes a hundred million-plus years to make should not be given away for a few mere dollars per gallon. When we run out, we can't just whip up some more. This is why this is a big problem. Every day it's getting worse, because every day we have less and less of a finite resource called petrochemicals, more people worldwide demanding their fair share of it, and no way of making more in time. "

Ashley and Brian felt the sense of doom pressing on their chests and found it hard to breathe. Gasping for air, they couldn't … catch … their … breath.

"You can see the problem, can't you?" asked Tommy.

All they saw was the problem. It pressed against every sense they had. It pressed hard on their eyeballs, which watered and cried until they couldn't see straight. When they looked at the trees, the trunks and branches now looked like the structure and piping of oil derricks. They saw themselves surrounded by oil derricks.

Moments before, the wind that howled through the trees had brushed the branches together in a rustling sound. Now it was suddenly a pulsing, thrusting sound of metal rods and pistons driving deeper into the earth through the action of the derricks. Their ears were filled with the clanging and banging until that was all they heard. It pressed on their eardrums until they couldn't hear straight. And everything they touched was slippery and oily and black and smelly until their fingers were saturated and they couldn't feel straight. They felt exceedingly gooky. It pressed against their noses, the heaviness of oil in the very air so thick they couldn't smell straight. It even coated their tongues and felt and tasted oily, until nothing else penetrated and they couldn't taste straight. The weight of it all was too much, so very much that now they couldn't think straight, and they were now more afraid than ever they were before.

Tommy waited until they were engulfed with fear, then spoke to them with fervor, confidence and assurance. "We have to drill to get more oil. We have to drill everywhere. And we have to get it before someone else gets it first. We need all we can get or we're done for—goners—you know what I mean. We need to store it and save it and hide it and hoard it. Before we do anything else, all our effort must be on getting all the oil."

"How do we do all that?" wondered Ashley.

"Oh, *you* don't have to do it," said Tommy with a beguiling smile. "We have people who will do it for us. They're totally focused on the oil. All they think about is the oil. They dream in oil. Oil is their magnificent obsession. They'll tell us what to do and how to do it, just the way it's always been done. It's exciting, don't you think?"

Ashley proclaimed, "No I don't! This feels gooky, stinky and yucky. I don't like this at all. I just wanna go home!"

"I want out of here now!" Brian piped in.

Tommy was not to be deterred. "Okay, okay, but let's go on down to Houston on the way home. It's just a hop, skip and a jump away." Tommy hopped, skipped and jumped over to a giant four-thousand-year-old sequoia. "Watch this." With that, he tapped three times on a knothole and the massive bark slid aside, exposing a glassed-in elevator. The back panel of the elevator revealed blue sky beyond. "Hurry up," Tommy gestured as he stepped inside.

Ashley and Brian hopped, skipped and jumped over and into the elevator. When they stepped inside, they noticed the control panel buttons were labeled Houston, Honolulu, Hamburg, Hanoi, Havana, Helsinki, Haikou, Hakodate, Halifax, Hangzhou, Harare, and HOME. Before the kids could dash to push "HOME," Tommy smashed the button for "Houston."

The elevator whooshed downward at hyperkinetic speed and pressed the flesh of their cheeks into a droopy distortion. With a shudder, the elevator jolted to a stop and the floor slid out from under them. For a moment, they hovered in mid-air. Suddenly three plush leather chairs rolled into place right under them and they plopped down and were instantly spun around three times in a blinding blur. They found themselves at the far end of a boardroom table of a major oil company. The glass walls of the conference room allowed a sprawling view of Houston.

Ashley and Brian both blurted, "Hello, hello—" and weren't heard by anyone. Brian jumped up, shouting, "Can't you see me?"

Tommy said, "No, they can't see or hear you; we're peering into another plane of reality."

"Then why are we here?" questioned Brian.

"To know how to think about things," replied Tommy.

"What things? We just wanna go home," blurted Ashley.

"I want you to see firsthand that the oil executives are working on the problem. We only have a few decades left of oil. Doesn't that worry you?" Tommy turned his attention to the executives at the other end of the table.

The executives spoke primarily about two things: more profits now and not having all the answers. They were exuberant and focused on their work.

First on the agenda was how to maximize their profits right now. This meant figuring out how to get China, India, Indonesia and Russia to buy and use more oil. "More profits now" looked good on quarterly profit statements and to the shareholders, and definitely meant potential bonuses for the executives. They were all hoping to earn a $400 million dollar golden parachute retirement package someday, when they left the company, just like Lee Raymond at ExxonMobil.

While the kids watched the high-stakes wrangling they noticed Pulse Smartpens sitting on the desk before their places, atop corporate leather notepads. They had never seen pens like these before. This incredible pen recorded and remembered everything the owner heard, wrote and drew. It allowed them to hear what had been recorded with a simple pen tap on their smart pads. The pen did all the legwork.

Though the kids were invisible to the executives, they thought the information they were hearing would be useful later on. They loved the idea of the Pulse Smartpen and thought at first it was some kind of magic, but the pens were real. All the executives had one. The pen was so intuitive that Ashley and Brian simply tapped "record" to hear all that the executives were saying. They didn't need instructions. They picked it up on the fly.

It was disappointing to hear that the executives didn't have solutions to the problem with oil. Ashley and Brian knew that their parents and a lot of their parents' friends were counting on somebody important, like these guys, to solve the problem and find the solution. They remembered how the big oil company British Petroleum had been so badly prepared for emergencies during the disastrous oil spill in the Gulf of Mexico in 2010. BP had been making so much money, it seemed as if they didn't care about spending money for safety systems.

Playing with the pens, the kids wrote and drew and thought about what was being said in the boardroom. They saw a digital readout panel on the pen, and an earphone hole. Across the digital panel scrolled some letters … little teeny, tiny letters that they couldn't read. They couldn't even see that they were letters. Something was there, but it was a miniature moving blur. Intuitively, both kids reached into the shirt pockets over their hearts and withdrew the *Fear Free Glasses.*

Neither Ashley nor Brian noticed that the glasses had changed. The lenses were different, having rested next to their hearts; they were now not as dark, less smudged. They had naturally progressed toward clarity, so vision through them was less distorted.

Responding to the continuing intuitive tinglings in their tummies, they slipped on the glasses and saw the words *put on your headset* crawl across the readout panel on each of their Smartpens. Surprised, they glanced at each other … and being kids, they didn't hesitate to follow this mystery message. With the earphones in their ears, they heard a familiar voice.

"Only you can hear me," said AO.

True to his word, the executives could not hear AO. They didn't turn at the sound to look at the kids, but continued to blather on about the fact that the world was running out of oil and they wanted to maximize all the profits they could and capture the last drop.

Ashley and Brian were worried about what would happen to them and their friends and their parents when all the oil was gone. What would they do for energy then? And shouldn't we all be doing something about that now? The executives spoke quickly about other energy forms, but spoke most fervently about making really big moola from oil *now*. They used words like *stinking, filthy rich*, and someone said *Get outta Dodge fast*, which they all thought was funny. And they planned to meet on an island called Cayman and *cash in*, wherever that was.

"Don't be alarmed," AO said. "We've been here before, with this same fear." The image of two bright eyes and a set of smiling lips scrolled across the digital readout panel of the Smartpen. "Tap the pen three times at the bottom of the pad, where it says *Record*."

Upon the third tap ... they were amazed and dazed, for they had transitioned through time and space and history instantly, with no sense of time passing. They could tell that they traveled a great distance by how different everything looked; yet they were not tired at all, not in the least. In fact, they were exhilarated, mouths agape, awestruck into silence.

When they had left Houston it was daytime. But here—wherever *here* was—it was nighttime. The dim glow of light along the streets was from street lamps fueled by *whale oil*. Ashley scrunched up her nose; it had a funny smell when you got too close.

They were magically somewhere in the mid-1800s, which they surmised quickly because there were no cars—only horses, carriages and dirt streets. Men and women wore layers of long clothing that went from their shoes to their necks with no skin showing except their faces, and the men covered most of their faces with beards.

Ashley and Brian looked at each other with the same thought: It must have taken forever to get dressed in the morning, to get undressed at night, and then to dress again in head-to-toe pajamas. The thought of it was exhausting.

It was also exciting, because though the scene before them looked like costumes and props from the movies, this wasn't a film set: There was nothing modern anywhere, and they didn't even carry cell phones! In fact, there were no telephones, no electric lines, no gas stations, no TV antennas—and the horses pooped right in the street. The kids were wide-eyed with amazement.

Two men were before them, men well dressed in black suits and long coats, wearing top hats. The tall one walked with his shorter friend, both deep in a serious discussion about the lights of America, which were about to go black because of hunting down all the whales. Soon there would be no whales or whale oil. The front page of the newspapers hawked by young newsboys blasted out the warning **AMERICA WILL SOON BE DARK** and fearful prophecies of **No Whale Oil, No Light**. The media fanned the flames of fear to sell papers.

A wisp of white fog curled around the lamppost like candy cane stripes and sparkled in the glow of the whale oil light. The lamplight flickered in strobe effects like that of an old-time movie. In the dancing shadows, the fog dipped and rose and bent and bowed until it twirled 'round the lamppost like a graceful dancer ... and stopped. The kids saw AO leaning against the lamppost with arms folded, wearing a silly grin and a glowing white, misty top hat.

"That was a little something I showed my friend Fred Astaire. He was a wonderful student, but that's not why we're here now. I want you to listen to these gentlemen. They're wrestling with a fear, just like you." AO then allowed Ashley and Brian to hear the timeless conversation in a way that they could easily understand, which was the way they would speak in their own time.

The short man spoke enthusiastically, with conviction and fiery excitement. "I have a solution! Black stuff is emerging from the ground in Titusville, Pennsylvania. I saw it yesterday. It smells bad;

it's thick and gooey and is not drinkable. Someone punched a hole in the ground trying to find water and found this despicable stuff. I tasted it and immediately spit it out. The ugly taste would not go away. And ya sure as hell can't drink it! They call it *the great black swamp*. It sticks to everything. It does have one funny property: it lights on fire and it burns hot, long and slow. It is like stored energy! It comes out of the earth continually, like that geyser called Old Faithful in Yellowstone."

"I brought home some of the black stuff in a canteen that I kept behind me on the rump of my horse, 'cause it smelled bad and made my eyes burn. I figured out how to break it into burnable kerosene, just like I refine booze, and it can be our future illuminant."

He jumped with glee and shouted, "Whale oil be damned, I can light America with this black stuff! I was up all night dreaming how to make a fortune with this. If we don't have whale oil, we'll need something. This is that something! Rock, I need you to work with me to make this the illumination of the future—and who knows what else it can do!"

The tall man listened with intense interest, digesting his friend's words.

"Rock, will you be my partner?" continued the short man. "I think this can become the energy source of all energy sources. Your friend Henry Ford has been getting a lot of press lately with his buddy Tommy Edison, who bodaciously said he can replace candles. Well, maybe Ford could run that newfangled horseless carriage with this stuff. You know what I think? I think it's black gold and it's going to be the standard for the world. And that's what we should call our company—Standard ... Standard Black Stuff. Rock, my boy, I promise you, we're going to make history!"

Rock hooked his arm around his friend. "I couldn't be more excited! You're right, Henry, with this idea we're rich already. We're just going to catch up to it. I can see it clearly even before it happens. Who knows, maybe we'll be the richest men in the world!

We've been masterminding for years, walking back and forth together to the office. *This* is our breakthrough. This is what we've been wanting and waiting for and dreaming, teaming and scheming for. We may want to re-think the name a bit. Someday they may name a plaza after me, and I'd rather it not be 'Black Stuff Plaza.'"

Ashley said to Brian. "Oh my God, that's John D. Rockefeller and it's called *Rockefeller* Plaza! And the other guy's his partner, Henry Morrison Flagler, who started Standard Oil and made Florida happen with railroads and agriculture and bringing all the rich people down to his place in Saint Augustine! I just studied 'em in American history class! Wow, I can't believe it, they're right in front of us—alive! I can hardly wait to get home and tell everyone! They won't believe it, either."

Ashley watched Rockefeller and Flagler walk by. She wanted to reach out and touch them and talk to them, but wondered if it would be like touching a soap bubble and breaking it. "I think they're alive—I mean, they're walking right by us," she said. "They died, didn't they? At least that's what my history book said, other-wise they'd be really, really old. Somehow this is happening now, right? Right in front of our very eyes, and we're alive. Aren't we? Maybe this is some weird quantum physics thing. We gotta ask AO how this works."

Brian said, "Wow! You know what that means? I read that his-tory repeats itself. History is repeating itself now, with another new energy shortage. I think AO wants us to see the reality or truth of it so we can tell everyone else. Just like before, there must be a solu-tion now too. We need a new energy source, just like they did then! And if it's renewable and sustainable, we won't run out this time! It requires brand-new ideas, ideas that no one's thinking or talking about or doing anything about. That's why AO brought us here."

"I got it, I got it," Ashley cried out, excited. "Where is that little shape-shifting white wisp when we need him? We gotta talk to him."

"I'm here, I'm with you always," said AO. Dancing out from behind the next street lamp, AO moved with the gentle grace and elegance of Fred Astaire and then with the precise power and poignancy of Gene Kelly, clicking his heels together three times in joyous glee. When he twirled to a stop, he struck a thoughtful pose in his misty white suit. Behind him, the fog formed an old Adirondack chair and AO sat, crossed his legs and now looked surprisingly like the late, great Mark Twain.

"You kids have got it!" AO said. "You are getting the message, and not one second too soon. I know that ultimately you both will be my messengers of hope, with insights and awareness critical to your future and that of your planet. The good that you must do can happen in the blink of an eye."

The whale oil street lamp flickered and light sparkled brightly from AO's white suit, causing Ashley and Brian to blink, just once. In a fleeting millisecond, their eyelids dropped down and bounced right back up, a single blink. They were astonished when they saw that AO was gone, along with the mid-1800s street and the whale oil lamps. And so were Henry Morrison Flagler and John D. Rockefeller. All gone.

Ashley and Brian found themselves back in the Houston oil company boardroom. "In the blink of an eye!" an executive shouted loudly. "The Gulf disaster happened in the blink of an eye! Now, how the hell're we going to stop something like that?" The executives still debated where to find solutions.

From his chair, Tommy looked over at Ashley and Brian and smiled. "Keep listening, you might learn something. I hope you've been paying attention. Have you learned anything lately?"

"We have," said Ashley. "Some really cool stuff."

"Yeah," said Brian. "Maybe we could tell them some of it."

Tommy shook his head. "Oh, I don't think they need any help from kids, but it's a nice thought. Just keep listening and learn from the big boys."

Undeterred, Ashley and Brian simply looked at each other and picked up their Pulse Smartpens simultaneously. They both had a flash of an idea—and they had it instantaneously, together.

Ashley began writing with great excitement. On the special Smartpen pad, she wrote: **We need an inexhaustible energy source that doesn't run out**. She tapped the pen on the section of the pad marked *record* and the words suddenly appeared on the boardroom screen. Brian quickly wrote on his pad: **Energy from the sun, wind, geothermal and waves**. He, too, tapped his pen on the *record button image* on the pad, and the words jumped onto the boardroom screen next to Ashley's sentence.

The executives looked up at their screen. No one knew where the words had come from. They looked quizzically at each other. Someone wondered aloud, "Maybe it came from upstairs," and gestured up to the top floors of the company building. No one knew for sure. "Maybe we should do something with this," posed another executive, and they all nodded.

Tommy turned to Ashley and Brian, not knowing that they had written the words, and proudly puffed up as he said: "Didn't I tell you they'd come up with something?"

Ashley and Brian were excited, knowing it was their suggestions. "Yeah, it's really cool how this works," said Ashley.

"What'd I tell you?" said Tommy triumphantly.

"I never would've thought this was possible," said Brian. "Can we keep these pens?"

Tommy wasn't listening; he was studying the screen and the mysterious words. "What on earth are they going to do with waves?" he asked scornfully, referring to the last word Brian had written. He frowned and drops of doubt dripped from his forehead. They landed on the boardroom table and flowed toward the executives. "That seems like a waste of time. That won't work."

The more Tommy worried, the closer the river of doubt droplets approached the executives, until they too were dripping wet with doubt, as if they had fallen into a swimming pool. One of them moaned exasperatedly, "The idea about the waves feels all wet. Maybe we should just drop it." Tommy nodded in agreement.

Disheartened at the turn of events, Ashley and Brian looked out the tall glass windows and saw a huge wave rushing toward them. At the front of the wave was AO, now dressed in rainbow-colored surfing shorts and hanging ten on a well-waxed Malibu long-board. He towed two empty surfboards, which swiveled when he swiveled, and cut back when he cut back on the wave.

"Now I'm going to show you something really exciting, okay?" asked AO.

"Okay!" exclaimed Brian and Ashley simultaneously. And the next thing they knew, they were standing on the surfboards next to AO and the wave was rolling out across the sea. The sun shone brightly and seagulls flew next to them, by their shoulders. Their attire was instantaneously that of seasoned surfers and they felt like pros on their respective boards.

Between their boards, two dolphins surfed next to them and squealed with delight as they darted about the wave. For Ashley and Brian, it was like being on the greatest roller coaster ride ever. The truly amazing thing was that they were not even getting wet.

"You're going to see two things that no one's ever seen before. You're going to see what recently caused the paradigm shift. Then I'm going to fast forward five years and show you what will happen when all these pieces fall in place—just like what you saw with Henry and Rock and the whale oil. Whales were over-hunted and harvested almost to extinction, just as today we've over-fished many fish that you've heard about, such as the Chilean sea bass, which is now almost extinct."

The kids were enjoying their rad surfer-dude duds and their agility and ability on the longboards, without a single lesson. AO surfed with the professional precision of champion surfer Duke

Kahanamoku, despite now wearing flowing alabaster robes over his surfing shorts.

"Do not worry about your clothing," said AO. "It will automatically change and be appropriate as we go from experience to experience. Pay close attention! You are going to take your world-changing insights and new revelations and use your Smartpens to communicate your newfound wisdom directly into the oil executives' minds, hearts, and souls. As you'll find out when you get back to the boardroom, the executives don't know where these solutions are coming from. They think they're coming from upstairs, or ... *Upstairs.* Remember, U R the solution, and like I said: 'I am with you always and in all ways.'"

With that, AO whisked Ashley and Brian forward to 2016 to a platform two miles off the shore of California, where tidal energy was being used to desalinate ocean water into pure drinkability by the company Natural Power Concepts. NPC's excess energy sent water forty-five miles inland to make the deserts bloom; it also helped to create abundant food for all and energized handsome-looking electric cars. As a result of this technology, oil was used only perfunctorily in this time, and the American economy was again booming and zooming.

"Belief is not just wishful thinking," AO said pointedly. "It is active. There is energy behind it. And it generates enormous results for the benefit of all. Right now there is a man who believes and acts on a high level. His inventions, which rise from his belief backed with the persistent action of a team, exist *now*. His name is John Pitre, and many consider him the Leonardo da Vinci of your time. He is the founder of Natural Power Concepts. You'll learn more about him later. What you should know now is that years ago he saw this solution in his imagination, and drew it as an artist. At first others scoffed and ridiculed and did not see the potential and wisdom of his ideas.

John prevailed, however, because he kept his focus on the solution and not the problem. He made models and prototypes; his belief in himself and his ideas attracted attention and investment, and are now the solution to the problem for everyone, everywhere. You, Ashley, and you, Brian, can take *your* beliefs to new heights. It is a choice you have."

Looking at John's inventions and the promising amount of clean, fresh, drinkable water gave the kids enormous hope and the belief that they could convince people, especially the Houston oil men, that there was another—and better—way.

"Once there are new choices, as you will see and hear, the seeds of doubt attempt to plant themselves. In sales it is called *buyer's remorse*," AO continued. "My friend Albert would tell you: 'If you keep doing what you've been doing, you'll keep getting what you've been getting.'"

Ashley and Brian were elated by AO's inspiring words and by seeing, right before their eyes, what was possible. This new energy platform was in natural balance with the ocean environment. It would never foul the waters with disastrous leakage of dirty, sticky, sludgy oil. It would harm neither the fish of the sea nor the fowl of the air nor spoil the beaches of man. Here was proof that being in harmony with nature was efficient, productive and profitable. Being in harmony meant operating with actions that blessed all and harmed none.

AO was delighted to see the joy on their faces. "So, I am going to get you back to the boardroom one second after you left it, so you can communicate more inspiring ideas with your Smartpens," AO uttered as he disappeared again, and the kids found themselves plopped into the plush Corinthian leather chairs in Houston.

Poised with his Smartpen, Brian wrote: ***The solution is be an alternative energy company with full services now, unlike the railroads, who thought they were in the railroading business***

and missed the gargantuan opportunity of being in the trans-
portation business.

Again the executives were perplexed, looking around the table at each other in trepidation and fear, wondering where the messages came from. "Who's writing this?" exclaimed one. "Anyone want to call upstairs and see if this is coming down from the Big Guy?" asked another. They all were too intimidated to volunteer.

Suddenly on the screen the following words appeared one by one: *This . . . is . . . coming . . . from . . . the . . . big . . . guy . . .* All the executives shivered and shook and held their collective breaths, while *. . .*

. . . Ashley finished writing with her Smartpen: *. . . so get to work! Discover how to make alternative energy—wind, solar, geothermal, and tidal—profitable* now, *before our competitors do. I want immediate implementation.*

Tommy noticed that it was Ashley writing the words that appeared on the board. Agitated, he began coughing, bringing dark misty dust particles up from his lungs and spewing them directionally at the man at the head of the table, who was in the middle of a speech.

"I guess one of the best ways to get alternative energy going is to —" he inhaled, swallowing a torrent of Tommy's doubt dust, and continued his speech: "—to … wait a second, wait a second, we've got trillions of dollars of oil at stake. We can't run off and just do alternative energy without first harvesting all the oil. That's nuts! We've got to launch an epic quest for oil, money and power! We are the biggest industry in the world."

The oil exec was back on point, setting himself euphemistically on fire, his excited peers watching him burn with eagerness as he clearly and emphatically stated, "Oil is the way, the only way."

"Let's get our PR firm to tout all the new alternative energy that we are developing, in order to keep the public hoodwinked and bamboozled. And let's get our pipeline and production chiefs on the phone and tell them to 'Drill, baby, drill!'" He smiled proudly and said, "We've got 15,000-square-foot mansions to keep, servants to pay, fat pensions, stock options, and consulting deals to wrangle, chauffeurs and chefs to enjoy, and we love flying on our own G-5 jets."

Tommy turned his attention back to the kids. His coughing covered their **Fear Free Glasses** with a dark, dirty layer of sticky soot. Their once-clear vision was again clouded with doubt and indecision, distorting their reality. No longer able to see clearly, the kids got up from the table and stumbled into each other, groping as if blind in the boardroom. Once again, they were forced to take Tommy's hand to find their way out.

Tommy led them into an elevator marked *Express*. Inside there was one button, marked *Forest of Fear Express*. He placed Brian's finger on the button, like teaching a two-year-old for the first time, and calmly told him, "Okay, Bri, let's go home."

Hearing the word *home* made Ashley and Brian less apprehensive. They were primed and open to suggestion. With a whoosh, the elevator rocketed downward and shuddered to a stop. Tommy took their hands.

The doors opened ... and a thick, gnarly forest spread out before them. The kids were unsure if they could even exit the elevator. A big, broad, ancient tree trunk was smack-dab in front of them, blocking their way. A heart carved on the tree held their names inside. An old, rickety wooden sign hung from a rusty nail driven into the bark. It read: *Tree of Indecision. It is here that all activity stops.*

*Your belief keeps you anchored
in the problem.*

The Possible *walks among us, though
many times unseen, unfelt and unheard.*

---

*Logic will get you from A to B.
Imagination will take you everywhere.
—Albert Einstein.*

CHAPTER FOUR
Seeds of Doubt

4

SEEDS OF DOUBT

Ashley and Brian waited for Tommy to move around the *Tree of Indecision*, but Tommy just stood there with them ... staring at the tree. They thought of him as their leader now; surely he must know the way around it. They didn't understand why they were still standing there and staring. After all, they thought of themselves as *young kids*, why would it be up to them to know how to get around the tree?

A snowy white finch fluttered onto a branch of the *Tree of Indecision*. Its little eyes darted back and forth from the kids to Tommy. With ease, the little finch lifted off the branch and flew around the tree, sweeping into and out of the elevator as if flying laps at an aeronautical race. He had no trouble getting past the *Tree of Indecision* again and again, lap after lap.

Of course, it's easy for the finch to get past the Tree of Indecision; he's a little bird, thought both Ashley and Brian. And one thing they knew for sure, they were not little birds. Finally, the finch fluttered back to the branch in front of them ... and opened its mouth.

Tommy heard the finch chirping and found it annoying. A deep, dark frown curled onto his forehead and mouth. Ashley and Brian did not hear the chirping. Not at all. Not one single *chirp*. For them, the sounds from the little finch were not chirping; the finch was *talking*.

"So you think you're just *young kids*, and Tommy is your leader and you're waiting for him to decide, and you're positive you're not a bird," said the voice from the finch. Ashley and Brian were not surprised to recognize the voice as AO. "Interesting, the labels you give each other, isn't it? Seems very natural to you. You call one person a king, another a pauper, someone else a genius or a dope; others you call successful, and some even failures. You call yourself something different, and so easily accept that that is who you are. Did you ever consider that these titles, these labels, disconnect you from each other and create a feeling of separation? The labels cause you to believe that you are 'this' and someone else is 'that.'"

"While Tommy is staring at 'this' and 'that,' I want you to put your glasses on and come with me for a second."

Both kids reached for their glasses and did not notice that the lenses were smudged and darkened. In the short, almost fleeting second it took both of them to lift the glasses to their faces and slide them onto their noses, the little finch flew back and forth between them, flapping its wings rapidly across the lenses to clean them.

The finch hovered in the air between them and they distinctly heard AO's voice say, "Do exactly as I do. Let's go." With that, the finch took off like a rocket around the *Tree of Indecision*. Ashley and Brian responded as they were told, and before they even were aware of what they were doing, they were flying circles around the terrible, trembling, troubling, treacherous *Tree of Indecision*. Tommy didn't see them, as they were moving too fast.

"***You are flying at the speed of awareness***," said AO, dipping and spinning and rolling with joy as he soared ever faster. "Your left wing is thought and your right wing is action. When moved together, you get somewhere fast."

When Ashley and Brian looked at their wings, nothing looked different, for their wings were simply their arms. With their arms outstretched, their wingspan was too wide to get past the *Tree of Indecision*, yet with each passing lap they slipped easily by the obstruction as if it wasn't there.

"Still think you're not a bird?" chortled AO. "It's amazing what you see when you stop looking with a limited view."

Both kids were enthralled with the experience of flying faster and faster ... until Brian wondered *How on earth do we stop?* He felt indecisive, and before he could blink he was standing stock-still in front of the tree, his way totally blocked, staring at 'this' and 'that' again through fogged glasses with Tommy.

Ashley completed three more fast laps around the tree until she worried where Brian was; did she need to save him from some terrible trouble? She blinked once and was standing next to Brian, her glasses now also fogged up again. The tree was still in their way and Tommy was annoyed.

"Look at this bird brain," said Tommy, referring to the finch. "Noisy little pest, isn't he? Whoever came up with that statement *'A little bird told me'* never listened to this racket!"

Ashley slipped her arm between the open elevator door and the trunk of the *Tree of Indecision*. It was a tight fit and her arm got stuck. She looked to Brian for help, but he had copied her and his arm was stuck also.

"So what have we learned here?" asked Tommy. "You can't do anything about a problem this size without a company behind you. A big company. Are you a big company? Do you have one behind you? No? Then what choice do you have? I mean, let's be real, you're just kids. Who are you to think you can solve this? Nobody expects you to, really, so don't worry! Someone else will handle it."

As he listened intently to Tommy, Brian noticed that his feet were stuck in gooey goop, as if he'd stepped into a big pile of wet, sticky chewing gum. He lifted his leg and stringy strands of slippery slop kept his shoe tethered to the ground.

Meanwhile, Ashley was not paying attention to Tommy. She was looking up at the top of the *Tree of Indecision*, wondering if she could climb over it and down the other side, though it stretched right up to the clouds. She realized then that she really didn't want to climb a tree. What she *really* wanted was to go swimming. It was hot in the small elevator. She thought of how wonderful it would feel to dive into the cool, clear water of a mountain lake. The very thought of it gave her goose bumps. She closed her eyes and took a few strokes in her imagination, in the crystal clear waters of a mountain lake.

She opened her eyes, turned to Brian, and said simply, "Let's go swimming." Joyful and expectant, she stepped forward and easily slipped past the *Tree of Indecision*.

"Swimming!" exclaimed Brian excitedly. "That'd be fun!" Seeing Ashley ahead of him, he called out, "Wait for me!" Propelled by his newfound enthusiasm, the chewing gum-like strands of goop snapped off his shoes and he ran past the *Tree of Indecision* to catch up to Ashley.

Excitedly, the flashy white finch said, "Rub your glasses over your heart as you run."

They did just that, and little wet smudge balls flew off the lenses into the air as they ran. The smudge balls didn't touch them, though they ran through a veritable rainstorm of the dark drops shed from their lenses. Instead, the smelly smudge balls splattered onto the branches of the trees in the *Forest of Fear* and melted, drooping downward, hanging from the branches like strings of mucky mucous.

Ashley and Brian ran with such delight at the prospect of *going swimming* that they didn't see any of the ooey, gooey, hooey hanging around them. To their amazement, as they slipped on their dimensional glasses, the ground ahead of them shimmered like a heat wave rippling off the desert floor.

It seemed that they were racing toward a mirage, nothing more than an illusion. However, this time they did not hesitate. There was no fear holding them back. They had no doubts about where they were going, no doubts because their hearts were on fire with desire. They were propelled by the power of joy. Why? They wanted to go swimming.

In their minds, they were already there. Thoughts of cool, clear water and the way it would feel pulsed through their entire beings. They vibrated with the energy of the joy of swimming. It was really that simple ... and there was no effort at all.

With nothing to hold it back from transforming, the shimmering mirage ahead solidified into a glistening, crystal clear body of inviting water, *The Lake of Imagination*. Serene, enticing and exhilarating, it beckoned them.

Ashley and Brian squealed with delight and raced to the water's edge. Excitedly they kicked off their shoes and laughed heartily to discover that they were already wearing perfectly fitting swimming suits. As they plunged into the water, they didn't notice that Tommy had disappeared behind them.

The water caressed their bodies with silky softness, enveloping them in undulating waves of joy. Their eyes were wide with amazement. Their **Fear Free Glasses** had instantly molded into **Without-a-Doubt Goggles**, and the underwater life was extraordinarily abundant and beautiful. Tall, thin, lush plants rose from the sandy bottom like strands of ribbons. They swayed in unison with each gentle surge of current, reflecting the dappled sunlight that filtered down from the surface, creating a rainbow ballet.

Fish of all shapes, sizes, colors and characters swam in and out of the rocks and plants in playful abandon. Their swishing sashaying and darting diving rippled the water, generating columns of bubbles that rose from their fins.

Each bubble was like a note of music. As Ashley and Brian swam through the concerto of bubbles, the tiny goose bumps on their arms and legs drew each bubble toward them like a magnet until each goose bump was connected to a bubble. The resulting connection filled the kids with a symphonic vibration of music. Most wondrously, it was not a hearing experience, it was a *feeling* experience.

Ashley and Brian were so enthralled with the ever-changing kaleidoscope of colors and the deeply felt music that they had not given one thought to the fact that neither of them had the need to take a single breath. They were just *being*. In this pure state of joyful being, they were once again like kids, and the worries of the world were only a faint and fading memory.

Into this watery wonderland of imaginative being swam a big old alabaster koi, pure white but for translucent pink eyes and bright orange tips on his fins and tail. Like a slow-motion hula dancer, he swished his body side to side through the water, and wiggled his tail fin when the tall dancing reeds tickled his tummy. He swam right up to Ashley and Brian and opened his mouth very wide. A single large bubble the size of their faces floated out and hovered between them.

Ashley and Brian were transfixed. The koi undulated from side to side in rhythm with the swaying plants but didn't move forward. It was like dancing in place. His mouth opened and closed; it almost seemed that he pursed his lips in a silly little smile.

This was alluring enough in itself, but the really captivating thing was the bubble. Inside the bubble were oodles of little alphabet fish swirling round and round. They were very ordinary looking, like bland guppies; they were called alphabet fish simply because all the other names had been taken.

Entranced and enticed, Ashley gently reached out her finger and touched the bubble. To her surprise, it did not break. It looked so fragile, but amazingly did not shatter. And then it happened, something even more astonishing. Something they had never imagined was possible ...

One by one, the bodies of the alphabet fish lit up from within—a bioluminescence that took the shape of a single letter. As if following instructions, the little alphabet fish swam into an orderly pattern facing Ashley and Brian, with their tails down and their heads up. The letters lined up into a sentence: *Imagination is the lake that holds all solutions.*

Brian wanted to take a turn at touching the bubble. He stuck his finger out, more impetuously and not quite as gently as Ashley, and jabbed the bubble. It still did not break. This time the little alphabet fish swam around in circles like they were racing, then screeched to a halt as if on cue. This time the bioluminescent letters said: *Dive in the bubble, swim around. Learn to fully use your imagination.*

What happened next was sudden, immediate actually, but that's because it was simple. Out of the pure joy of the desire to play, Brian effortlessly imagined himself diving into the bubble to swim with the alphabet fish. Ashley watched with her mouth agape as Brian dove into the bubble, which was only the size of his face. Inside the bubble, he was now much smaller.

Brian stared at the alphabet fish ... he was exactly their same size ... and they stared right back. Without warning, they zipped off and swam around him at dizzying speeds, then slammed to a stop in a straight line. This time their bodies lit up from within and the lighted letters spelled out: *Hi Brian!*

Brian stuck his arm up to wave *hello* to the fish, but he was too near the top of the bubble and his hand poked through, protruding back into the lake water. The bubble did not burst, which was amazing, but the most truly amazing thing was that his hand was now its normal size again—yet the rest of him, inside the bubble, was still small.

Ashley grabbed his hand and tried to pull him out of the bubble. Brian had no idea his size had changed; he was having too much fun and didn't want to leave the bubble yet, so he pulled Ashley toward him. Her hand poked through the bubble and she saw that her hand was now very, very small. She quickly pulled her hand away from Brian and out of the bubble, and was relieved to see her hand was its normal size again.

Inside the bubble, Brian did gleeful somersaults with the alphabet fish, feeling like one of the master acrobats in Cirque du Soleil. Their bioluminescent bodies spelled out *whoa!* and *whoopee!* He discovered that if he thought it, it became so. He wanted to stay inside the bubble and impress Ashley by doing cartwheels around the inner edge of the bubble's circumference. Brian opened out of a spinning somersault with his arms and legs splayed in a spread-eagle pose. His hands and feet protruded from the bubble and were NORMAL sized, but his body was teeny tiny inside the bubble.

Ashley burst out laughing, spraying the lake water with funny bubbles because Brian looked so silly and ridiculous. The big alabaster koi with orange tips was laughing too.

Brian, intrigued by what the fish did, decided he would entertain Ashley in a similar fashion. At the speed of thought he became a flashing purple and yellow neon sign, saying: *Hi Ash, come on in, your imagination is fine. Think it and you'll be mine.*

Now Ashley wanted her own bubble. It seemed like so much fun. In her laughter, a small bubble burped from her mouth and expanded until it enveloped her inside. Sublimely simple and swift.

Surprised, Ashley looked around and saw a rainbow. Unlike the crescent-shaped ones on land, this was a fully spherical, multidimensional experience of colors on the rim of the bubble's translucent surface. There were no fish in her bubble, which did not worry her because she had not really wanted fish.

She'd been thinking of really cool clothes, outfits that she'd always wanted. Suddenly, she saw those very outfits floating by inside the bubble. When she touched one with her finger, she felt a slight jolt of electrical current and the outfit morphed right onto her like a second skin. She touched another outfit and another shock covered her in a second outfit, replacing the first.

She did this again and again, and it was the most fun. She could've continued this all day. She was surrounded with floating clothes when she heard a voice rumble through the water like a resonant, rippling vibration.

"What is the largest nation in the world?" the authoritative voice asked.

Brian pulled his hands and feet back into the bubble, growing tiny again, and searched for the location of the voice. He saw no one. In the water, he knew the voice could have traveled from a great distance. He looked at Ashley and saw that she didn't see anyone either, though clearly she had heard the voice. Both kids shrugged.

"Don't duck the question," the voice rumbled through the water.

Ashley and Brian both felt its vibration go right through them. It tickled and stuck to them like an itch that couldn't get scratched.

"What is the largest nation in the world?" The vibration of the voice was now all around them. It seemed to come from every direction.

All the alphabet fish stared at the koi, who stared right back. Then they all turned and stared at Brian and Ashley. It was a bit odd and a bit unnerving.

Ashley opened her mouth and said, "Russia?" Brian piped up, "China?" When they heard no response, they both quickly tried, "The United States?" Still no response.

"No, no, no. Those are all way too small," the voice vibrated. "This nation is much larger and it's in each of you, each of us, and in everyone, everywhere. This is the most important geography to know."

Ashley and Brian didn't know what this *other* geography was. Then the alabaster koi swam up toward their bubbles. With one swish of his tail, he caused a current that bounced the two bubbles into each other. When the membranes of the two bubbles collided, their surface tension broke. Ashley's little clothes gushed out into the lake and dissolved. Brian's alphabet fish floated away as soggy letters. The two kids looked at each other. They were normal size. They stared into the round eyes of the alabaster koi.

"The largest nation in the world," said the koi, "is ... "

"AO!" blurted Ashley. "It's you!"

"You're a fish?" asked a stunned Brian.

"I'm whoever I want to be," said a very pleased-sounding AO. "And I'm glad you're beginning to recognize me. Thought it'd be hard to hear underwater, didn't you? Thought I'd be all muffled, I'll bet? The fun part is that you're not hearing me with your ears right now. They're full of water." AO laughed through his gills.

"But I do hear you, I know that," said Brian.

"You can see me in an infinite number of ways, if you want," AO replied. "You don't always have to hear me with your ears or see me with your eyes. Expand your sense of how you *see* and *hear* and *touch* and *smell* and *feel*."

Ashley *heard* his words as a *vibration* in her heart, then as a *gut feeling* in her tummy, and she was really surprised when the *goose bumps* on her arms seemed like sounds. "It's really fun," grinned Ashley.

"Of course it's fun," agreed AO, speaking with a definitively British voiceprint. "It's supposed to be fun. A lot of people forget that. That doesn't worry me, though; it's their choice. You can limit how you see, smell, feel, taste, and hear me, yet you can't limit me."

Brian also was amazed at how easy it was. When he closed his eyes, let go of all doubts, and simply expected to see AO, he saw AO swimming right in front of him. "I see you, I see you!" shouted Brian excitedly.

Ashley checked to make sure Brian's eyes were closed and waved her hand in front of Brian's face.

"I see you, Ash, you're waving at me." Brian had a big, triumphant grin sprawled across his face. "It's so clear; it's like a really strong feeling."

"That's because you're living in the largest nation in the world right now," said AO.

"I am?" Brian still didn't know where that was.

"You both are," said AO, sounding suddenly like Yoda. "Now let me continue with your geography lesson. The largest nation in the world ... is ... is ... your *imagination*."

"Is that koi comedy?" quipped Ashley.

"Only if you laugh," chuckled AO. "*Imagination* is a real nation. You need to visit it often. You don't need a passport or a visa. You don't need to ask anyone, even a parent, for permission. You just go inside your mind. Your imagination is the most marvelous, creative capital of the universe. It is more important and real than facts. All invention, innovation, and ideas come from it. Imagination is one of the most powerful forces that the world has ever known. It separates you from all other animals. With it you are in touch with the infinite and thus, unlimited. You can use it to break through any and all barriers. With it you can go over, under, around or through any wall or detour. Imagination is exciting when you *feel*, like you just did, that you can use it to your unending advantage, instantly and constantly."

AO added, "Love is your imagination in action, at its best."

Little pieces of crystallized water floated by them, like individual snowflakes; they did not melt, were not absorbed by the water embracing them, but rather danced within it. The crystals initially all looked the same. They were homogenous, with no differentiation, and at first glance somewhat boring.

AO said to the kids, "I want you to morph the crystals. Think an angry thought and watch what happens."

To their amazement, the crystals turned an ugly, putrid yellow and took on irregular, sickly looking shapes.

"Now, think a loving thought," AO directed.

They did. With glee in their eyes, they watched as the crystals shape-shifted into perfectly symmetrical hexagonal shapes in white-pink and translucent lavender. They looked like impeccable snowflakes. AO let them enjoy the floating cascade of beauty for a moment.

"I would like you to know of my friend, Masaru Emoto, from Japan. He took photos—maybe you saw them on your internet— showing the transformation of water crystals when exposed to music, words, emotions or thoughts, like you just did, that are either empowering or devouring."

"It was really easy to make a beautiful crystal," said Ashley. "I want to do more."

"It was also easy to make an ugly one," remarked Brian.

"Yes, just by what you were thinking and feeling," said AO. "Think about that for a moment. If thoughts do that to crystallized water, imagine what the water then does to you. Your physical expression is made up of about 60 percent water."

"I don't wanna make myself ugly inside like that," exclaimed Brian. "No way!"

"And I wouldn't wanna do that to someone else, either," added Ashley.

AO was very pleased with the direction of their thoughts. "Imagine if you could take water right from the air, or air right from the water? Or take polluted water and turn it into clean, instantly drinkable pure water?"

"That would be fun," said Brian assuredly.

AO nodded in agreement, and then to keep them on their toes mentally, he asked, "What would Tommy say about that?"

Their foreheads wrinkled and their mouths scrunched up, squeezing the fun right off their faces. It was clear they were worried about what Tommy might think. They didn't want to make a mistake, they thought. They didn't want to seem dumb. This vibration of fear brought fear back and gave it form. Their thoughts gave it gravitas, a weight in their experience. The mere invocation of Tommy's name harkened back to all his concerns and his rigid and regimented thinking and—bingo! Tommy reappeared.

Now in full scuba gear, moving ungracefully through the water, Tommy proudly struggled to reach them, out of breath and huffing and puffing, grumbling and groaning, regretting the effort to swim fast enough to catch up to them. Ashley and Brian were surprised that Tommy was there in the twinkling of an eye, with a water voice translator in his regulator mouthpiece that gave his voice a dissonant, icy tone that chilled their bones.

"You called?" Tommy was ready and willing to be of service, as long as it was all about him. "How do I look? It's the latest rage, a red suit with black tuxedo piping on the legs. Everything you need to be underwater, which makes me invisible to color-blind sharks." Tommy didn't seem to notice that the kids had no gear, nor did they seem to need any.

"You sound all muffled," said Ashley.

"Of course, I'm muffled. Like you, I am underwater," said Tommy. "You might wanna put on some scuba gear." Tommy couldn't believe they hadn't thought this through. Under his breath, he muttered, "Kids, you gotta teach 'em everything."

Tommy adjusted his face mask, exhaling and purging it, and red-rimmed bubbles surged to the surface. The kids noticed their distorted and discolored shapes, hissing with heat and emitting a rotten egg stench.

"To answer your question," Tommy said, "the one about taking water from the air, it's real clear—that's never gonna happen. Air is air and water is water. Anyone can see that."

The koi swam around Tommy's red-hot air bubbles. The movement of his fins churned the water, banging the bubbles together and creating an unholy sound like a clanging cymbal, off-key and tonally distressing.

AO said, "Tommy, another limiting thought, hey? Where is your expectation? Is it on good? Or is it doubts, heavy with fear? Expectation is a powerful state of being. It can be powerful in the right direction."

Tommy stared at the "talking" koi, astonished. He turned to Ashley and Brian with a look of grave disappointment. "I leave you guys alone for one minute and you're talking with a fish. Do you know how stupid and ridiculous this looks? Fish don't talk, and if they did, who'd want to listen? All they do is spit and fart bubbles."

"Wait a second," said Brian. "You just heard him."

"Heard who?" queried Tommy.

"Me, that's who," AO said, rippling the water, his deep, bass voice echoing with a Doppler effect in the wet environment. "I am here, that you can hear. Do you hear me now? Yes, in my present form, I am a fish, a koi. I can be bigger."

AO became the size a great white shark with eyes black as coal and pearly white teeth sharp as razors. When the shark smiled, Tommy could see his own fear-stricken face reflected back at him in each mirror-like shiny tooth. "Does that make you happy?"

Tommy cowered and shivered, repulsed with fear.

"Or I can be smaller," said AO, as he morphed into a guppy-sized fish. "Or I can be a blue whale, the largest creature on the planet."

Instantly, he was magnificently huge, so huge they could not see around him. AO spoke with the deepest and most resonant voice that anyone had ever heard. He slapped his blue whale tail and the entire lake shook, throwing sand and driftwood up on the shore. He certainly had their attention.

"As I was saying," AO reminded them, "you could take water from the air. Many places are experiencing a shortage of water because of the way they are dealing with things, but they always feel an abundance of air. The truth is, there is an abundance of water, and an abundance of all things, IF you know how to positively and correctly use your imagination."

Tommy grunted. "Of course there's an abundance of air, except underwater. This is why most of us don't spend a lot of time down here." It was hard for Tommy to talk with the regulator filling his mouth, and his oxygen tank was nearing empty.

"Right!" said AO. "You know that another name for water is H2O, Tommy. That means that water is, in fact, one part air." This seemed like a very impressive fact, coming from a hundred-foot-long blue whale.

"You *can* take water from the air,'" AO continued. "The idea started in imagination, which turned into realization. When you get back home to your computers, check out my friends at *Skywater* because they're already doing it. Their machine separates the moisture from the air and provides drinkable, pure, abundant water, enough to make the deserts bloom, just as it was predicted in the Bible more than six thousand years ago."

"I've never heard of them," stated Tommy defiantly.

"Ignorance is not a very good defense of one's belief." The whale swished his tail and Tommy was sent cascading off in a torrent of current. AO turned back to Ashley and Brian. "When you're ready to take a step, then the doubts seem to flood in. This is where most people live and where momentum slows or stops. *Fear is not a fact, if you are willing to act. Act through your fear and it will disappear.* If you *really knew* that infinite good was always available, you would fearlessly take the first step."

AO swam off toward the far reaches of the lake, constantly morphing into new shapes ... jelly fish ... squid ... turtle ... mermaid ... then Pegasus, rising from the water propelled by his wings and soaring toward the sun.

Tommy had breathlessly managed to swim back to Ashley and Brian, but his wetsuit had been turned backward from the turbulence of AO's whale tail. His face mask was now upside down and half filled with water.

"You know," Tommy said, "he's trying to get you to *feel* right about things, instead of taking the time to learn all the facts and then *know* you're right. You have to learn everything there is to know before you know what to do."

"That could take a long time," Brian thought.

"Time well spent," praised Tommy. "You see, you don't listen to your heart, 'cause you're smart and don't want to get taken advantage of."

Both kids thought about whether they really believed that to be true. They knew others believed that way, but they realized there was a fear tucked into that thought. Maybe they didn't have to accept that fear as fact.

"It's really just a suggestion, isn't it?" Ashley thought out loud.

"Yeah," chimed in Brian. "What if we don't believe that?"

Tommy looked at them with grave concern. "That's how people get fooled, with pie-in-the-sky hopes, and then they get flummoxed, foiled and fleeced. Haven't you ever heard of people who got lost in their imagination, following their heart? Some of them never came back to reality."

The more Tommy spoke, the more Ashley and Brian noticed that the level of the lake was receding. The water was draining as if someone had pulled the plug on a drain, and a whirlpool of water spiraled slowly downward.

"You kids ..." Tommy continued as they all began spinning round and round and down and down in the whirlpool of water. "You kids don't realize the impact and import of collective consciousness. That's like the thinking of everyone, added together. There are just some beliefs that everyone believes and you get swept along with them. You can't fight it."

The harder Ashley and Brian tried to swim out of the whirlpool, the more it held on to them. The lake was draining fast, ever downward.

Tommy was really on a roll with his pontificating. "It's like that sage advice, 'You gotta ride the horse in the direction it's going.' That's what they say and they say it for good reason."

Ashley and Brian were getting dizzy from spinning around in the water and whirring 'round and 'round with Tommy's words. Tommy was unconcerned that the lake was almost gone. He merrily blathered on. He didn't imagine anything differently because he knew that this was how things were—everyone believed this was the only way things were. They were always 'this' or 'that,' there wasn't something else. "What you see is what you get" was collectively accepted.

The kids listened to all that Tommy was spouting—and he was certainly spouting with great confidence and a grand sense of authority—until they found themselves spinning on the sandy lake bottom with all the water leached out. Everything was now dry as a bone as far as the eye could see. Tommy's wetsuit and scuba gear were useless and his swim fins were filled with sand.

Shimmering in the heat of the day was an old, rotted, wooden sign peppered with worm holes. In faded letters it read *Great Desert of Despair.* Beneath these words were smaller, ominous words in tiny letters: *Prepare to Despair.*

"Brian, what're we gonna do?" Ashley wondered anxiously, as Brian stared at the vastness of endless sand. "How do you prepare for that?"

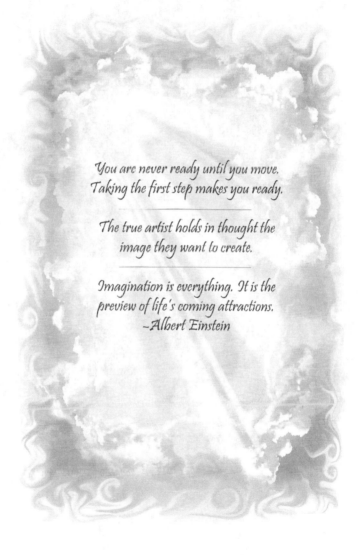

You are never ready until you move.
Taking the first step makes you ready.

The true artist holds in thought the
image they want to create.

Imagination is everything. It is the
preview of life's coming attractions.
–Albert Einstein

CHAPTER FIVE
A MacGyver Moment

5

A MacGyver Moment

Standing in the sand surrounding them and up to their ankles, with their **Without-a-Doubt Goggles** on top of their respective heads, Brian said, "Remember, AO taught us to put our glasses on after rubbing them over our hearts. Let's do it now."

With some trepidation, due to Tommy looming ominously like a vulture ready to eat its dying prey, Ashley bravely took off her **Without-a-Doubt Goggles** and rubbed them over her heart three times to clean them, and Brian quickly and assuredly did the same. Both were instantly wowed by the results. To their astonishment the goggles not only became clear again, they became glasses. They felt an inner vibration that was good.

They put on their **Fear Free Glasses** and saw the desert had bloomed. They were dressed again in the clothes in which they had begun and were apparently in a safe place, with only their memory of the sinking, swirling sand that had been sucking them into a black hole in *The Lake of Imagination.*

Both kids were astonished at what they saw. The stark nothingness of the desert had been replaced with blooming life all around
them. Ashley removed her glasses for a moment and once again
saw the desert wasteland spread before her as far as the eye could
see. The more she stared at it, the farther it stretched. It was almost
hypnotic. This was clearly a problem. She didn't want to walk
through an endless desert; yet try as she may to see a way out, the
more she stared at the desert, the more desert she saw.

This is what most people saw when they stared at a problem and
wanted it to go away, but instead it just grew bigger. Ashley knew
instinctively at this moment that she needed to look at her circumstances differently. She tilted the *Fear Free Glasses* up in front of
her eyes again and saw a clear path lined with flowers and flowing
water. It was actually a river of great and exciting possibilities.

"Brian," she called out excitedly. "We have to tune ourselves to
what we want to do. It's like listening to the wrong radio station;
we just have to turn the dial to what we want, to get what we want!
If we are tuned to the wrong station, say polka music, the station
may be great for someone else but terribly useless and uninter-
esting to us."

"I could use a drink of water," said Brian. "It's hot out here. And
I don't see any water." Brian saw only the endless sand; he had
taken off his *Fear Free Glasses* to wipe the sweat from his face.

Tommy stepped up, took the glasses from Brian's hand and
wiped them on his shirt, turning them darker, like sunglasses. He
handed them back to Brian. "Here ya go. You're gonna need a good
pair of sunglasses out here in the hot desert sun." He reached over
and did the same for Ashley. "You too, Ash. That bright sun's not
good for your eyes; doctors recommend that you always wear your
shades in the hot sunshine."

The darker glasses now shaded their eyes from the sun, but they
no longer saw what was really there, at least not in its entirety. Now
they saw a distorted view, and this distortion became their new

reality. However, they had been given a glimpse of what was really there, and the memory of AO's words remained with them. They needed to look at the solution rather than the problem. The problem was no water and only sand, everywhere they looked. The solution was water, but it took a degree of faith to look for it, because they could not see it with their eyes.

At this point, the water was only a vision in their hearts. They knew from AO's words that faith created hope, and hope generated momentum, and momentum provided progress, and progress got them closer to experiencing what really was.

Confidently, Ashley said, "There is water here."

"Yeah," agreed Brian. "Something around here should help us."

Tommy looked around completely bewildered. "There's nothing but sand."

"We just have to look at the sand differently," said Ashley. "What else can we do with it?"

"I can put it in a sandbox, which seems kind of silly as I look around. I could use it to make a beach, if I had some water! That's our problem, remember? No water! Just sand!" Tommy was really frustrated.

All of a sudden, Brian was wrapped up in a memory surging through his consciousness. His face lit up. "I remember my dad telling me about a company he had invested in called Mia Solé. He was really excited about it. They had a photovoltaic process that used silicon to make a solar cell out of sand—and we've got a lot of sand! They also use copper, and Ashley's got a copper bracelet. They add a few other things and then kind of squish it all together in manufacturing to turn the sun's energy into pure energy. They can use this energy to power all sorts of things… like air conditioning, which would be cool right about now."

Tommy looked around with a sarcastic squint to his eyes. "Do you see any manufacturing plants around here to 'squish' things together?"

"Well," Brian pondered, "if I had just one of those four-inch solar cells, I could use it to bounce heat from the sun onto the curvilinear bottom of my Technomarine watch and cause fast condensation that would drip into our mouths. We wouldn't be thirsty anymore! That'd be a really cool MacGyverism, wouldn't it?"

"Wow," Ashley exclaimed excitedly. "We could use a lot of those solar cells to generate the energy we'd need to run a machine that could pull water from the air."

"Oh now you're talking about magic again," griped Tommy.

"No," said Ashley. "You just don't remember. AO told us about *Skywater*. They have a device that takes quality water right out of the air with instantaneous filtration. They use pure oxygen to vaporize all contaminants, and it tastes great. This isn't pie-in-the-sky hopes, it's actual real water from the sky. And with Brian's solar cells, we'd have essentially the free energy to run it, even way out here!"

Tommy chimed in, "That's all well and good, but we don't have all the material here with us to power the *Skywater* thing and we don't even *have* the *Skywater* thing. No one's going to deliver to us way out here, so we still don't have any water. So that idea is nothing!"

"It isn't nothing!" argued Ashley. "Ideas are things. Ideas make stuff. They cause solutions. They're new possibilities. The Bible talks about making the desert bloom, and the only reason the people didn't do it then was that they didn't have the belief and were not aware of the ideas. But the ideas were there and they were real. And these ideas that you say are nothing are solutions that are changing our world for the better!"

"Yeah, yeah, yeah, but we're still in the desert!" Tommy emphasized sarcastically.

"Well ..." Brian thought carefully, "maybe we don't have to be."

"Yeah, yeah!" realized Ashley excitedly, when she sensed where his thinking was going. She took the dark glasses off her face and rubbed them over her heart three times. Brian watched her and did the same. Ashley stared at Tommy. "I don't want to be in the desert anymore, how's that grab you?"

And in the next instant, she wasn't.

Tommy couldn't see her anywhere. "How'd she do that? Where'd she go?"

Brian slipped on his glasses and saw that Ashley was right next to him and that rivers of flowing water were gushing in front of them. "She's right here. She didn't go anywhere." Ashley and Brian leaned down and drank of the cool, glistening, sparkling water until their thirst was quenched.

"I read where all reality is parted from us by the flimsiest of screens, in the **Be Here Now** book. And those glasses from AO are the flimsiest of screens. I think we just jumped time and space realities," said Brian.

"You jumped realities alright," said AO, riding up behind them on an alabaster camel with pink eyes, clothed in the white flowing robes typical of a Bedouin sheik. "All your realities are a belief, and this is a better belief, and so a better reality. I congratulate you both."

He dismounted the camel, who then bent his long neck down and nuzzled AO's face. "Thank you, my good friend," AO said as he patted the muscular neck of the desert beast. "Great fun, as always." AO turned to Ashley and Brian with a twinkle in his eye. "I just love this outfit. I've had it for years. Rapello and I," AO said, referring to the camel, "were extras in the movie *Lawrence of Arabia*."

While he spoke, AO loosened the straps from a large pack on the back of Rapello. The camel knelt down on his front legs to lower his back and make it easier for AO to undo the pack.

"I hope you know," AO continued, "that good movies and books and stories can make you aware. They connect you to the world around you. They hold up a mirror to show you who you are. They are a powerful way to move your culture forward."

AO unfolded the corners of the pack and it popped open, rising up and reconfiguring into a white tent that stood on its own, without support stakes or guide wires. It looked like it might be big enough for the three of them. "Come on inside, I want to show you something."

He opened the flap of the tent and beckoned Ashley and Brian inside. They had to duck to get inside, pushing aside the tent entrance flap. When they stepped into the tent, they uttered a sigh of wonder and awe. From the outside the tent was only big enough for three, but inside the space was cavernous. Huge white canvas walls rose up before them on all sides and the top was as high as the sky. But this wasn't even the most impressive part.

More astonishing were the images of *Lawrence of Arabia* that were projected across the white canvas walls. They felt as if they were in the middle of the desert, surrounded on all sides. The canvas walls shimmered in the blinding heat of the desert and dis-appeared to their eyes. The only part remaining was the tent entrance flap, seemingly standing up on its own. The rest of the tent had vanished. They now felt as if they were in the middle of the movie itself ... which, actually, they were. Peter O'Toole looked down at them from atop a camel! The camel bleated!

Outside the tent flap door, Rapello responded with his own bleating reply. Ashley and Brian looked behind them and saw for themselves that the tent door was the only part of the tent still standing. The flap over the tent door parted, pushed aside by Rapello's nose, and he ducked down and walked into the movie with them.

"Rapello," said AO, "come say hello to some of your old friends."

There were now camels and Bedouin soldiers everywhere. It was all happening so fast that the kids didn't have time to be afraid, for it all felt like such fun. They couldn't help giggling with delight.

Brian was astonished. "Is this happening now?"

"To you it is," said AO.

"You mean we're really in the movie?" gasped Ashley, and ducked as a camel galumphed by her, stirring up the desert sand.

"Yes, you are, and you're watching a miracle," said AO.

"I thought we were watching a movie," said Brian, now confused.

"No, we're *in* the movie, that's the miracle," exclaimed Ashley.

"The miracle you are watching, the one I want you to see, is not the movie or being in the movie, but is the miracle hidden within the story of *Lawrence of Arabia*. It was considered impossible to unite the Arab tribes for any reason. They could never cooperate and get along with each other. This was a truth known for centuries and, sadly, it is still true in many ways today. But for this moment in history, T. E. Lawrence, a British soldier, showed what was possible when people work together."

Brian kept staring at the tent door flap. What was on the other side? Even with the movie action all around him, he was curious and just had to see for himself. He opened the flap and stepped out, to the other side.

He found himself next to the flowing river waters from which he had drunk only moments before. Gone were the Bedouin soldiers and camels. Gone also were Ashley and AO. Only the tent door flap remained, standing by itself. Brian called out, "Hey Ashley, can you hear me? Where are you?"

The tent flap was pushed aside and a gust of swirling desert sand gushed out ... and Ashley stuck her head out, followed by AO's head, and then Rapello's big head. "What do you want?" Ashley sounded a little annoyed.

"I just wanted to make sure you were okay. What're you doing?"

All excited, Ashley's eyes lit up. "We were charging across the desert with all the Bedoiun tribes. What are you doing?"

Brian looked all around. He saw no charging army, no camels, just the door flap with their three heads sticking out. "Not a whole lot, but you'd be really surprised what it looks like from over here."

Curious, Ashley walked out from behind the tent flap, followed by Rapello and AO. She turned and saw the tent flap standing on its own, like a portal back into the magical world of *Lawrence of Arabia*.

"Wow ... far out," said Ashley.

"This is very trippy," exclaimed Brian. "Just like the Sixties."

"This movie was made in the Sixties by my good friend David Lean. It's one of the great movies of all time and a grand lesson in human behavior."

"The Sixties ... wow," said Ashley. "Rapello must be really old for a camel."

"No, he's quite young at heart, actually," replied AO. "Rapello decided not to believe all that gobbledygook about getting old. He decided to stick around and keep having fun. And we've been doing that, haven't we, my good friend?" Rapello nodded his head up and down in agreement.

"Maybe he could give us a ride back home," suggested Brian hopefully.

"You'd have to tell him where to go," said AO.

"You mean he doesn't know?" said Ashley, discouraged.

"Well, has he ever been to your house?" AO stared at the kids as they thought this one through. He waited for their answer.

"Ahhh, I don't think so," said Brian. He looked at Ashley, who shook her head *no*. Brian realized that his chances of going home hadn't gotten any better because of Rapello. He also noticed that camels have a really bad smell.

AO could tell by Brian's scrunched-up nose what he was thinking. "It might be interesting for you to know," AO said to both kids, "that you two don't smell real good to Rapello either. He just decides not to let it bother him that you're different and don't smell like a camel. It's more important for him to like you. It makes him feel good."

Ashley reached out and stroked his long leg. "He really likes us?"

"He does," said AO. "And he'd take you home if that's how you want to go home."

"How far is it?" asked Brian.

"How far do you want it to be?" responded AO.

Ashley knew that camels could go a long way without water, so if Rapello was willing to take them home it must be rather far away. The thought of it made her sad. "I didn't think it would be that far, but I guess we've walked a long way. We've been through forests and lakes and deserts. I haven't seen any houses in a long time."

AO looked at them with great affection. "Here's something I'd like you to think about. You were able to step into a small tent and be in the desert with Peter O'Toole and Omar Sharif. Then you stepped back through the tent door that stood up by itself and were back here again. This probably isn't something that happens to you everyday, would you agree?"

Both kids nodded in agreement.

"Yet because you haven't seen any houses in a long time, you think that it'll take a long time to get home. That's what I would call 'conditioned thinking.' You have let the conditions dictate how you should think about things."

"But that's what we know." Brian tried his best to defend Ashley's position.

"And how do you know that you couldn't step back through that tent flap and be right there in your front yard, right now."

"Could we do that?" Ashley said suddenly excited and hopeful. "Could we really do that?"

"Not the way you are thinking," said AO. "In order to do that, you have to think differently about what's all around you. You have to see things differently than the way you've been conditioned to see them. You have to be expectant of miracles."

"Miracles only happen every once in awhile, that's why they call them phenomena. We want to go home now. We don't have time to wait for a miracle," said Brian dejectedly.

"That's only because you expect miracles to be rare and unnatural." AO was most kind and patient with their fears and doubts. "If you look at things differently, you will see that miracles are natural occurrences. They don't look natural to you only because you're not at that vibration level. Awareness will open up a whole world of miracles."

Brian was still confused. "An awareness of miracles?" he asked. "What's that?

AO smiled deeply. "I'm so very glad you asked. It means that your desire has sparked. Perhaps it is only a tiny spark right now, but the tiniest of sparks can ignite a fire. And when your desire is on fire, it burns away lingering doubts, revealing the miracles that await you."

The kids watched in amazement as AO paced back and forth in front of them, utterly enveloped with enthusiasm, his feet never touching the ground. The more thrilled he was with the principles he evoked, the higher he rose.

"This could be a turning point in your lives and for your planet," he stated with profound assurance. "Every good story has a turning point. If you embrace the truth within these words, the story of your lives will turn from the path of the ordinary to the miraculous."

Ashley and Brian were captivated by this thought, because AO's enthusiasm for it was rooted in a joy he wanted to share. He so fervently believed this to be so, it was as if he wanted to give them the kingdom, to hold nothing back from them. It was indeed his good pleasure to be doing this.

"There was a time in your history," said AO, "when miracles were accepted and expected. The Bible, and other ancient texts preserved from numerous cultures, spoke of those for whom miracles abounded."

AO sat into the lotus asana yoga position with his legs crossed —but he was not sitting on the ground before them. He was levitating, actually floating in front of their faces as they stood listening to him. Both kids had the same thought at the same time: *This was like a miracle in motion.*

AO continued his enlightened and elevated discussion. "You must reach back and take hold of the miraculous thinking of ancient times. From the hallowed halls of antiquity are true tales of those who had not educated themselves out of miraculous thinking. Remember, at one time in your history, highly educated people were absolutely convinced that the earth was flat and if you were not careful you would sail right off the edge. You will find examples of this same kind of education today, concerning things that are thought of with such assurance and confidence, yet years from now will be found to be far from the real truth of things.

"You now think that the medical procedure of *bleeding a patient* to cure illness is barbaric. But it was once widely embraced by the wisest physicians and even practiced on George Washington, the first president of the very new United States of America. In fact, the doctors placed so many leeches on his body to thin his blood and suck out the illness that it actually hastened and brought about his death."

AO paused to make sure they were listening closely. "When future generations look back on your current time, how barbaric will they find the widely-accepted practices of *chemotherapy* and *radiation* for dealing with cancer? Limitation of belief and acceptance of those limitations in the collective consciousness has you at the point in your so-called advanced and modern era where you no longer accept miracles. However, in ancient times, supposedly not as advanced or wise as present day, miracles were natural and expected occurrences. You must become aware of miracles happening naturally every day. This awareness will expand your world beyond your wildest dreams. Your universe is in the expansion business for each and every one of you. Nothing is withheld except in your own limited thought."

"What do we need to be aware of?" asked Ashley.

"That the world around you is not limited. That what you see is not just what it looks like. That there are many possibilities in the simplest of things."

"The simplest of things?" she asked, not quite grasping his concept.

"Yes," AO replied assuredly, "the things which are right before you. This is what I call *having a MacGyver moment.*"

"Are you talking about the TV character?" Brian wondered.

"Yes, from the television series of the same name, *MacGyver,*" said AO.

"Starring Richard Dean Anderson?" said Brian.

"One and the same," smiled AO.

"My mom thinks he's really dreamy," said Ashley, "and I think he's cute."

"If you remember," continued AO, "MacGyver took the simple things which were right in front of him and used them as solutions to the problems he faced. He found many uses for a paper clip beyond holding sheets of paper together. He knew that a discarded gum wrapper was not merely trash, but could be used to conduct electricity. For MacGyver, the thin filament inside a broken light bulb was not something that was no longer useful because it could not produce light. It could be used to pick a lock, and possibly many other uses that he knew he could become aware of and utilize."

"What if you don't know as much as MacGyver?" Brian was suddenly worried about his own perceived shortcomings. "What if you haven't learned all those things? How do you become aware of something you haven't studied, or something you don't know?"

AO was pleased with Brian's thinking. "I'm glad you phrased it that way. When you listen again to what you asked, you will realize that you are approaching the situation by concentrating on what you are lacking. *Think of how differently you would feel if you started off thinking that you were connected to all the answers and that anything was possible.* Now that you're starting from the point of where you want to go, it's not as far to travel, is it?"

"You mean start at the finish?" asked Ashley.

AO nodded. "If you start from the premise that everything is already all right, then fear doesn't get in the way of your awareness of the solutions. The important thing to remember is that Mac-Gyver knew all these things not because he studied more than you, but because he never allowed himself to feel trapped. He never accepted that as his reality, regardless of what the circumstances might want to dictate. He knew ideas were an infinite realm of possibilities. It's a different way of thinking."

"Different from what?" wondered Brian.

"Different from how most people confront a problem. They start from the premise that they lack something; it could be simply the answer, or maybe the tools to help solve the problem. Then they struggle and sweat to find or create what they need to fill their 'lack-gap.' What they're missing or lacking is where their attention is focused, and that's a very narrow focus that prevents them from seeing all that they have. *If you start from abundance, realizing that the solutions are all around you and ever present, your thinking expands from there to an awareness of the possibilities that before were invisible to you.*"

"Then you look at everything differently," Ashley said. She was getting excited about what this could mean. "You're not as worried. A problem becomes an opportunity to experience how the abundance of solutions will manifest themselves for me today, instead of just a problem to worry about."

"This is it, exactly, Ashley," said AO admiringly, in a British accent. "When you are open to all that you have, you start thinking differently about that paper clip and discarded gum wrapper at your feet because they could be keys to the solution. When faced with a problem or trapped by circumstances, like MacGyver was many times, how much do you want to limit yourself? Do you believe in solutions? Solutions abound. History is filled with stories of people who saw what was already present, but that no one else could see until they focused a light on it. Then it seemed so obvious that everyone exclaimed, *Why didn't I think of that?*"

AO uncurled his legs from the lotus asana and stretched them down to the ground. With his feet coming back to earth, his thoughts turned to the practical aspects of what he had been telling them.

"Many solutions literally and figuratively lie in the trash—those things and ideas that we discard because we think they have no value for the problem we face. This is the *MacGyver* concept of looking at a paper clip and realizing that it very possibly has infinite uses. Your beliefs keep you anchored in the problem, if you let them. You fear it's too big, too complicated and feel trapped. You can't get out. MacGyver saw that solutions are all around you. He never accepted being trapped. ***He felt empowered and confident from within***, because what was out there no longer scared him. The *MacGyver* thought process cuts through the fear to the solution. Start from this enlightened premise, and then *MacGyver* your way from the ideas to the manifestation of your solution."

Brian was pumped up with excitement. "I can't wait to tell some of this to Tommy when we see him again. He's been a bit of a sourpuss and this may feel pretty good to him."

"I'm glad you want to help others, Brian," said AO. "That's a lovely quality and one never to forget. If Tommy chooses to not believe in what we've been talking about, that's his choice."

Ashley shared her concern with AO and Brian. "Sometimes when I'm around Tommy, I forget what I want to think about and end up going along with what he's thinking, doing, and saying."

"You always have the ability to decide which thoughts to accept. Be alert and catch your thinking when it falls into a *lack-gap* trap. Let me give you an example."

AO extracted two mechanical pencils from inside his robe and pulled the erasers from both pencils. He reached down and picked up a handful of fine, powdery dirt. Slowly, he poured the dirt into the open top of both pencils. As the dirt flowed into the pencils, Ashley and Brian noticed that the granules were actually little letters and numbers. When the pencils were filled to the brim with letters and numbers, he jammed the erasers back into place, dropping a few letters and one or two numbers in the process.

"Now, take a pencil," AO commanded. Ashley took the first pencil and Brian took the second. "Are you ready to write?"

"What do we write on?" Ashley looked around for some paper.

From within the deep recesses of his robe, AO withdrew two yellow pads of paper. "Use this for now. Maybe later I'll show you *air writing*."

"*Air writing?*" Brian wanted to try that now. "Could we try—"

"Maybe later, but for now just use paper." AO stood quietly for a moment. His face took on a serious expression. "This will be a test."

Both kids tensed a little, pencils poised. Their breathing quickened like horses in the starting gates at a race track.

"I want you to write as many big words and large numbers as you can, as fast as you can." AO suddenly looked concerned. "I hope you each have enough of the right letters and numbers in your pencils. You wouldn't want to run out at the wrong time."

Both kids became nervous, contemplating the possibility of running out of letters and numbers. They gripped their pencils tighter.

"Get ready," AO suddenly said. "Get set ..."

Both kids waited in breathless anticipation.

"Go!"

Ashley and Brian wrote furiously on their yellow pads. They used letters and numbers, a lot of them, and just kept writing and writing. Suddenly Brian's pencil slipped from his hand and dropped to the ground. The eraser top came loose and bounced away, and Brian watched in horror as letters and numbers poured onto the dirt and were absorbed out of sight.

"Oh no," said Ashley, very concerned, "what are you going to do?"

"I don't know," Brian said, extremely worried.

"Are you afraid you'll run out of numbers and letters?" AO waited patiently for an answer. "Do you think you may have a *lack-gap* of numbers and letters? What about you, Ashley? Do you now have more than Brian?"

"What happens if he can't find enough letters and numbers?" Ashley was concerned for Brian. "Can I give him some of mine?"

"Am I going to be in trouble? I didn't mean to spill all those letters and numbers." Brian looked at AO apologetically.

"Do you think they're lost forever?" asked AO.

"Well, I saw them disappear into the dirt and I don't see them anymore." Brian looked down at the dirt at his feet where he had spilled. It just looked like dirt.

"How soon before you run out, do you think?" AO quizzed them.

Brian looked up at AO then down into the empty darkness of his pencil.

"Can you tell how many of the letter 'a' you have?" AO asked. "How about twos and fours, do you have enough of those?"

"I can't see any," said Brian as he squinted down into the pencil. "What do I do if I run out?"

"***Ask better questions***," stated AO simply.

Both kids studied AO's face for a clue as to what he was talking about. But AO's visage was a benign stare, giving away nothing.

Suddenly Brian had a thought. "Is this like *Wheel of Fortune?* Can I buy a vowel or a consonant?"

"Maybe," replied AO. "You'd need a lot of money, wouldn't you?" Brian was stumped. "Better questions are free, however."

Ashley thought for a moment. She could see that AO was not mad at them. He was not upset that Brian spilled his letters and numbers. She reasoned this through for a moment, and then posed her question. "Why are we afraid of running out of numbers and letters?"

AO smiled. "That's a very good question, Ashley. And what's your answer?"

"You told us we wouldn't want to run out of letters and numbers at the wrong time." Ashley suddenly realized the connection. "And we accepted that belief, didn't we? We let fear in and believed we might not have enough. We created our own *lack-gap*."

"Yeah, but wait a minute," said Brian. "I saw the letters and numbers fall out my pencil."

"What did you see? What is a number? What is a letter? Is it physical?"

"Well ..." Brian contemplated for a moment. "Not really," he continued. "It's an idea, so I guess you'd say it's spiritual. So I suppose what I saw was a material symbol representing the *concept* of a number or letter, but the real letter or number was always spiritual."

"That's very good, Brian. And you've already seen examples of this, in which you instinctively believed. In school, when your teacher erased a number or letter from the blackboard, did you think they were destroyed and lost forever?"

"No," replied Brian. "I guess I looked at this limited condition and believed it to be true. I forgot that you can't run out of numbers or letters. We have an infinite supply, if we're aware that they're spiritual."

"So why do so many people get worried and say '*I've run out of ideas*'?"

"*Because they accepted limitation instead of abundance as their natural state*," replied Ashley.

"That's right, and if they change the way they look at things, the things they look at will change as well." AO was very pleased with their progress. "*Your Divine Source constantly supplies you with an infinite array of ideas.* They are spiritual and thus ever present. The minute you describe your world in material terms, you begin to ascribe limits to it—and belief in those limits 'carves out' your sense of reality. Think about this, the next time you look at your checkbook balance, or think about sources of energy or even the thought of answers and solutions, anywhere you are experiencing a lack-gap. *Decide to look at it differently and Mac-Gyver your way out.*"

"Can this work every time?" wondered Ashley.

"It is always working because it is the truth of things. You, however, may not always be fully aware of this. Each moment that you are more aware, you experience progress. When you see things differently, from a new or more enlightened perspective, you become aware of possibilities that before were invisible to you. Your reality is now enhanced, broadened and deepened.

"Reality hasn't changed. It always is what it always was, but now you see more of what was always present. U R the frequency you connect to, which allows for the evolution of your soul. *U R the solution or U R the problem, but either way ... U R.*

"Each day, each moment, you stop along the U R dial at the frequency U R w*hat*? The '*what*' is your choice. If you are not attuned to the frequency of your higher self, you are out of tune with the infinite. When you tune in to the vibrational frequency of infinite possibilities, you are invincible and unstoppable, no matter the challenge. When you are truly aware of this, your world will change in ways you never before imagined."

You must become, in thought and feeling, what you wish to live.

Where is your expectation focused? It just might be where you end up.

CHAPTER SIX
Clouds of Awareness

6

CLOUDS OF AWARENESS

Inspired by all that AO had been telling them, Ashley asked, "We can use these principles to get home, can't we?"

"You can use them for that and for so much more," replied AO.

Brian looked at his watch with consternation. "I hope we can do it quickly."

"*There's always enough time for the expression of good.*" AO let that one sink in for a moment. He didn't rush the kids. He didn't say another word.

Ashley and Brian knew this was probably important. Under their breath they each repeated to themselves, "*There's always enough time for the expression of good.*" Ashley smiled; it made her calm. Brian, not quite in the same mental space as Ashley, glanced at his watch and looked at AO expectantly. "Have you forgotten we want to go home?"

"Home is wherever you are," replied AO.

This did not serve to assuage Brian's concern.

"My dear friend, Bucky ..." AO paused and smiled, then continued. "Well, I should say, R. Buckminster Fuller, but I really loved calling him Bucky, and he preferred his friends to do so ... anyway, Bucky said *'Home is wherever I am on Spaceship Earth.'* I would tell him, as I tell you now, that home is wherever you are in your mind."

Ashley was smiling, but Brian's face showed no signs of breaking into a grin. It barely hovered above a grimace.

"Brian," said AO warmly, "are you happy in your mind with me? Have you had fun doing the things we've done, the places we've been, the people we've seen?"

As Brian recalled everywhere they had been and all that had happened, his lips unfroze and haltingly curled into a hesitant smile. There were still some doubts hanging from the tips of his lips like restless, persistent, pesky monkeys, but as Brian stared at AO's beaming face, he was soon helpless to stop a grin from bursting out ear to ear.

Both kids were sporting silly grins, offering pure proof that this was a look that would never go out of fashion. It would always be ultra cool and hip to love life. In the distance, they heard a sound of a different sort.

The clatter of galumphing hooves on the earth drew closer, and the dissonant chatter of an ongoing tirade against the problems of the world rose into the sky. Tommy was on his way ... astride a mischievously rambunctious Rapello. Tommy bounced and slid up and down Rapello's hump like a nauseous, drunken, seasick sailor. By the time Rapello arrived in front of AO and the kids, Tommy was hanging down from Rapello's neck with his feet dragging along the ground. When the camel stopped, Tommy collapsed into a heap.

"This beast ... is the most ... ungodly form of transportation known to man!" Tommy heaved out the words in gasps. Rapello turned toward AO and opened his mouth in a big wide grin.

Tommy caught his breath and continued, "I was stuck out there, wherever *there* was, all alone, except for this stupid camel. What I needed was a ride, and instead, this bombastic bozo of a beast began chasing me."

AO chuckled and glanced at Rapello. "Did you consider that maybe he was offering you a ride?" Rapello winked at the kids and sauntered off in search of new fun, utterly unconcerned with Tommy's misperception.

"Did *you* consider," blathered Tommy, "that this animal probably has a brain the size of a protozoa? Anyway, when I finally stopped running to catch my breath, out of the corner of my eye I saw him kneel down—he was obviously exhausted—and I knew instinctively that was my chance."

"That's how he lets you climb on for a ride," stated Ashley simply.

Tommy was not listening—except to himself—as he ranted on, "I latched onto his neck and swung myself up on top. For twenty miles, maybe fifty, even a hundred, he tried to throw me off, but I proved I was certainly his master because here I am. I can now tell you unequivocally that the camel is a gross mistake of nature. It is no less than a race horse designed by committee. Now, there are a few things I want to get off my chest."

Tommy proceeded to pull one legal pad full of notes after another out of his shirt, where they had laid plastered against his chest. He struck an orator's pose and began reading from his pads. "Look at the problems that have descended upon us, they are as plentiful as the grains of sand on the beach. What is to be done about this abominable mess? Let's talk about it, stir it around, see what we can find, dissect and analyze it and ... "

As Tommy continued, AO leaned over and whispered to the kids, "You might find this interesting. Stay alert and see what you think."

The first thing they noticed—it was impossible to miss—was that the environment around them was suddenly crowded. Animals of various species advanced on Tommy as he continued his diatribe, oblivious to the hordes of beasts approaching rapidly. "And furthermore," Tommy continued, "I see no end in sight for the calamities we must endure because of ..." On and on, he moaned and groaned his cacophonous complaints.

Like stagehands quickly changing the scenery of a play, the animals brought equipment, furniture and props with them. Three golden eagles swooped out of the sky, each clutching a wall in their talons. They set the walls down around Tommy. Through the opening of the missing wall, a rhinoceros thundered forward to shove a table with three holes in it in front of Tommy. From under the ground, three microphones were propelled from the earth by two gophers and a groundhog and pushed up through the holes in the table. Tommy now spoke into one of the microphones, and the other two awaited his guests.

Oxen pulled a wagon full of equipment that was rapidly unloaded by a crew of chimpanzees. Nails were pounded into the walls by spider monkeys sitting atop giraffes' heads to reach the high places, and pictures were hung on the walls by darting and diving sparrows, in an aerial display of acrobatic maneuvers. Television cameras were pulled into place by Great Danes, who then stood up on their hind legs and acted as camera operators. Little Chihuahuas darted around carrying cups of coffee and cartons of bagels and donuts. A radio station control console was butted into place by a trio of rams, and a gorilla took his spot at the controls.

When everything was in its place, a fourth eagle flew in with the last wall, which contained several doors. Tommy now was encased inside a fancy TV and radio studio. An orangutan led Ashley and Brian to the guest chairs and microphones, and they picked up headphones that had been positioned by a group of ducks. No sooner had they sat down and donned the headphones when a golden retriever wearing a *Media Maven* T-shirt brought over a book entitled ***Endless Arguments to Have****.* Ashley tossed it aside, not wanting to argue endlessly, and the dog brought it right back. Brian then threw it away and the dog brought it back again. This never stopped. And neither did Tommy.

On and on he ranted—about Wall Street and Main Street—liberals and conservatives—unemployed Americans and overpaid foreigners—government and business—the economy and crass entertainment.

"What do we do about the lousy liberals and all their social and environmental causes that are going to bankrupt businesses everywhere?" He pointed a finger at Ashley, demanding a response.

"Well, I think ..." Momentarily taken aback by Tommy's abruptness, Ashley recovered and offered a solution. "Maybe if we didn't label them as 'lousy' but realized they were concerned citizens, we could find a basis for common ground and begin communicating in a healthy dialogue that may—"

Tommy cut her off. "You can't communicate with someone who doesn't see your point of view." He pointed an accusing finger at Brian. "And tell me what are we going to do with all those crazy conservatives who want to save our country by getting rid of anyone who doesn't believe the way they do or doesn't worship in the one and only right way?"

"Perhaps," Brian began thoughtfully, "we could expand our sense of love and find the good in everyone, and then—"

"Then what would we argue about? We've got five minutes before the next commercial break. Do you expect us to just sit around feeling good about some satisfying solution that might actually work? What do we do after the commercial? We've got a lot of commercials here, pal!"

The golden retriever brought ***Endless Arguments to Have*** back to Brian. He dropped the thoroughly slobbered-on book in Bri's lap and wagged his tail, wanting more and more and ...

"You just want to agitate and irritate," said Ashley. "You really don't want a solution. That might hurt your ratings. It's better to keep everyone riled up. You want us to endlessly go 'round and 'round in the problem. You only want to generate ratings by using fear and anxiety to keep everyone on edge. You've done nothing more than create an addiction that serves your profit."

"We can always turn you off, can't we?" Brian considered doing just that, then stood up and took off his headphones. "Wow, it feels much better not having that noise in my head. Let's go, Ash."

Ashley took off her headphones and they both walked toward the exit. They looked back at Tommy to see a torrent of words flowing from his mouth, like a river that poured right into the microphone. Words began spewing from the speakers on the walls and spilling onto the floor. They had to push aside the growing pile of words just to get to the door. Finding a clear path was getting harder with each step, because some of the words were *slippery* and they lost their footing. Some words were *sticky* and their shoes scraped along the floor. Some words were *big* and *heavy* to push aside.

As they trudged through the rising tide of words, they knew that their decision to leave was only one aspect of a solution. The vastness of the problems created a sense that it was all so complicated. Maybe Tommy had a point after all, because there were so many choices to consider that might make a difference. How *do* you decide, they wondered?

AO joined them near the studio door. In the background, Tommy was having a grand old time talking away to whoever would listen as words continued to fill the studio. While AO and the kids spoke, a janitorial crew of chimps with shovels began piling words into wheelbarrows.

"How did that feel?" asked AO.

"Uncomfortable," said Brian.

"Not much fun at first," admitted Ashley. "But it was liberating when we left. Tommy's really got to *MacGyver* his thinking and try something else if he wants to feel better."

"And you just learned that your ability to feel better was always right there where you were, and available to you if you simply acted upon it." AO smiled proudly. "You didn't take his bait and get caught up in his endless cycle of swimming in the problem. The problem will always be a big deal for him because he never stops talking about it, complaining about it, and thinking about it. He doesn't leave any room for the solution to come into view."

"Shouldn't we talk about the problem so we don't ignore it?" asked Brian.

"Only enough to determine that it isn't where you want to go. Then you can walk in the direction of the solution, which is where you want to be anyway. You did ask a very good question, Brian, for it contains something to consider carefully. Ignoring a problem is not a solution. Ignoring a problem is being *in*active. You want to be *pro*active. Life is active. To be vitally alive is to be active, in thought and in action. You want to be proactive about the solution. Activity within the problem only stirs up the problem."

"Then why is the media so enamored with broadcasting those things that keep everyone riled up? Why do they always play in the dirt? Didn't they ever grow up?" Ashley was clearly perplexed. "They reach so many people. They could be a powerful force for solutions and for uplifting mankind. Why does so little of that appeal to them? I don't get it."

AO looked back at Tommy, who was jumping up and down in a frothing tirade at the microphone. "Some people in media see only the money. Right now, they are making a lot of money shouting at everyone and dragging the dirt, the blood and the fears into everyone's living rooms. Because fear can be contagious, many people have become hypnotized by the drone of the media message. There are many right-thinking people in the media who endeavor to change the tenor of this conversation with the public every day.

"There has been a shift in the corridors of creativity. A corporate mindset has taken over and is, for this moment in time, crushing creativity. The thinking used to be that good stories and good programming would make money because people are drawn to what is good and willing to pay for it. Today, however, making money is the measure of what is good or moral or worthwhile. Fifteen years ago, the television networks would have been appalled at the idea of putting on reality shows that celebrate backstabbing and deceitful, immoral behavior, but now they rationalize anything as acceptable if it makes money. Making money, by whatever means and with whatever content, makes anything right. It's a dangerous game of thought and the only way to win is not to play."

"Is it possible for things to change, even when they're making so much money?" Brian asked with a hopeful look in his eye.

"Yes, Brian," replied AO. "The same solution that is available for you is right there for anyone who wants to see it and live it. When you see things differently, from a new and more enlightened perspective, you become aware of possibilities that before were invisible to you. Your reality is now enhanced, broadened and deepened. Reality hasn't changed. It always is what it always was, but now you see more of what was always present. I've said this before and I might very well say it again."

"So much of the problem still seems awfully complicated," said Ashley, becoming distressed as she tried to grasp a sense of where to start. Even getting out of the studio seemed complicated.

There was a door in front of them, an old oak door with strips of embedded iron running along its edges as decoration. It was not the door one would expect in a modern TV and radio studio. The two other doors were modern, but they were five feet off the ground and required a stepladder in order to reach them. That, of course, seemed excessively odd, but they did look more like normal doors.

"Where should we go?" asked AO.

"Well, I guess the simplest way would be to walk through the old wooden door." Ashley looked at AO for any further suggestions. There were none forthcoming. "Is that right?"

"Makes sense to me," said Brian. "Remember KISS?"

"The rock guys with painted faces?" asked Ashley.

"No. Keep It Simple, Stupid."

"It *was* a simple question. Are you calling me stupid?" Ashley was a little peeved.

"No, the letters—K,I,S,S—stand for Keep It Simple, Stupid." Brian quickly replied. "You're weird 'cause you're a girl, but you're not stupid."

"And *you're* not weird?" prodded Ashley.

"I like being weird," beamed Brian. He turned to AO. "Can we go through the old door?"

"You can if you want," replied AO.

And they did. Pushing the heavy door open, they stepped through it, only to have its weight pull the creaking wooden door out of their hands to close behind them. At first there was only shadowy movement in a darkened room, until their eyes adjusted. What they saw then was not at all what they expected.

On the other side of the door, the rays of a setting sun sprawled across the floor past their feet and ran up the far wall. The window that let in the sun was a simple stone arch, open to the air, without glass or a structure for closure. Candlelight danced along the other walls and the sound of a struck match drew their attention to the far corner as another candle was lit.

The holder of the match was a man wearing a cloth tunic cinched around his waist with a knotted black cord, a hood folded down his back at the neckline. The top of his head was shaved in a pattern that looked like someone had put a bowl on his head and drawn a line around it, then gotten rid of all the hair inside the line. He wore sandals on his bare feet.

The walls surrounding them were stone and it was cold. A simple wooden table with one chair was the only furniture in the room. When Ashley and Brian looked around for AO to ask him where they were, he was nowhere to be seen. The strange-looking man with the funny haircut ambled toward them with his hands folded in front of him.

"Welcome, my children," he said simply.

"Why does he think we're his children?" Brian wondered if the man was lost and confused, or maybe a prisoner here in this cold, dingy room.

"Maybe we stepped into some kind of dungeon and we're slaves now!" Ashley was not happy with this possibility.

The strange little man had overheard them. "Nothing as complicated as that," he said. "You are my guests. And you are welcome. My name is William. And who are you?"

"I'm Brian and she's Ashley, or you can call her Ash and me Bri."

"Where are we? Is this part of the radio and TV studio?" asked Ashley.

"What is a radio and TV studio?" William inquired.

"You don't know?" asked Brian. William simply shook his head. "Wow, that's weird. What do you do if you don't watch TV?"

"I don't know what a TV is or why you would watch it, but I do spend a lot of time reading and meditating." William smiled benignly at them. "And of course I spend many hours writing philosophy upon the parchment at that table."

"Oh, cool," said Brian. "Is parchment one of the new versions of an iPad from Apple?"

"I have an apple to eat, if you would like one," stated William. He picked up a crinkled and curled piece of old yellow paper. "This is my parchment."

"Where are we?" asked Ashley, realizing that things were clearly different here and that William wasn't exactly up on what's new.

"You are in Occam, my village in Surrey," he said. He was aware that they looked at him with a fair degree of ignorance. "In England," he continued after a moment.

"How did we get to England?" whispered Brian to Ashley.

"I don't know," whispered Ashley. "You're the one who wanted to go through that door."

"I didn't know it went to England!"

"So, William," said Ashley, "I'm sorry I don't know your last name."

"William of Occam," he replied.

"Of Occam?" asked Brian. "They named the whole town after you?"

"I'm simply William," he stated. "And I'm from Occam and I am a friar here in the abbey."

It suddenly dawned on Ashley what was really happening. "What year is it?" she asked.

"It is thirteen hundred and thirty in the year of our Lord." William said.

"Oh boy," realized Brian. "This could be a problem."

"Why?" asked Ashley.

"Because they had really lousy toilet paper then and I may need some soon."

"Just hold it 'til we get back. Can you do that?"

"*If* we get back," Brian said with a worried look on his face.

"I have some thoughts for you, since you seemed confused about what to do," said William. "When confronted with multiple solutions to a problem, the choice that offers the fewest new assumptions yet still satisfies your inquiry is usually the best."

"Choose the simplest one, it is usually the best," realized Ashley. "That's Occam's razor."

"Sometimes you will discover that simplicity can be hidden by complexity. You hear too many stories instead of the *one* your heart is always telling you. You need to shut out the outside noise to hear the simple inner truth, the wonders within. Have faith, child, that you will find your way. Faith is awareness of what is, but not yet seen. You must see it in your heart and feel it, before it will manifest as a solution."

"So how do we know what is simplest?" Brian wanted to know. "Is it the easiest?"

"Not always the easiest, no," said William. "What I find most helpful is to use the sense of simplicity to look for the underlying principle. That principle should then be your guide. This is where the concept of the simplest path is most effective, when it illuminates the operating principle."

"What's the simplest way out of here? You must know that," said Brian.

"You could try the door. The window is also a choice, a faster one, but the ground is more than one hundred feet below and the moat is filled with alligators." William smiled pleasantly. "I've always preferred the door."

"Door sounds good to me," stated Brian confidently.

William guided them through the lengthening shadows as the sun dipped to the horizon and the candles burned low. He placed his hand upon the iron latch of the door and dispensed one more morsel of advice before creaking open the heavy wooden door.

"God's work is doing what you love," he said. "This is the simplest of guides and stands upon the most stalwart principle. The purpose of life is joy. We are here to create awareness of and access to more freedom for yourself and others. Once you have awareness, you must take action."

Encouraged by this guidance, they stepped across the threshold of the ancient door, expecting to be back in the TV and radio studio. Their expectations were once again dashed, for they found themselves in a backyard in California. They saw a *Los Angeles Times* newspaper on a small table on the patio with a date twelve years earlier. They were still trapped in the past and had no clue how to get home.

Ashley pointed to the date on the newspaper. "I was just a baby then!"

Hearing someone coming toward them from inside the house, they hid behind a hammock. A pretty blond woman stepped out of the house onto the patio. She was distraught, upset about something, and wiped tears from her eyes as she picked up the paper. She was also clearly scared. It was not a fear of immediate danger. It was the fear of not knowing what to do next, where to turn for help or how to move forward.

Ashley and Brian thought that at any moment they would be discovered, because the young woman walked right toward the hammock. They knew they were going to be caught in her backyard with no excuse and no idea how they got there. Brian decided to try complete honesty. He hastily stood up from his crouched hiding position and faced the young woman with as much courage as he could muster.

"Hi, I'm Brian," he said, hoping that would break the ice. "And hiding next to me is my friend, Ashley."

Sheepishly, Ashley slowly stood up, now that Brian had given her away. "I wasn't really hiding, I was tying my shoe, sort of, well maybe I was hiding just a little, but I didn't really mean it … "

The woman didn't respond, but she was certainly upset.

Brian stammered ahead with his speech of truth. "We're sorry we're in your backyard without asking first, but we didn't know that we'd be here because you see we were with William of Occam in this abbey in fourteenth-century England, and when we walked out of the door to his sanctuary we thought we'd be in this TV and radio studio but somehow we ended up here, so it really wasn't our fault but we're really sorry anyway if it's upset you."

"I know he sounds like a blithering idiot," added Ashley quickly. "And sometimes he is, because he's a boy, but this time he's really telling the truth, and I'm really his friend, and I wouldn't lie to you either."

This didn't seem to impress the young woman at all, because she looked right at them … and didn't see them. Brian and Ashley first thought she was really mad and simply ignoring them, but then they thought …

"You're right," said AO. "She can't see you." AO was now standing beside them.

"How did you get here?" asked Ashley.

"I've always been here," said AO simply.

"I'm going to have to look for you more carefully from now on," said Brian, somewhat annoyed that he had not seen AO before this moment.

"Well, realizing I've never left is a good place to start." Then AO smiled that warm and inviting smile that made them feel that all was well. "Makes it simple when you think about it that way. Might even be comforting."

Ashley looked at the young woman who seemed to look right through all of them. "Is she blind and deaf, is that why she can't see or hear us?"

"Oh no, not at all," said AO. "Her name is Jennifer McColm. She can hear and see and speak quite well. We are looking at an impression in time of her recent past. Every moment in time is like an energy wave that continues to flow. We are standing in the path of that wave and that is why you can see her, or see her as she was twelve years ago. She can't see or hear us because we are in our present thought construct."

"Why is she upset?" asked Ashley.

"What's she scared of?" added Brian.

"She's afraid she might lose everything she has: her house, her ability to feed and take care of her three children, any sense of a normal life."

"Oh my goodness," said Ashley. "What happened?"

"Her husband has just left her and Jennifer will soon be divorced. She has no job, no immediate prospects of a job, and no idea of what kind of job to look for. She only has enough money for nine months and she has a lot of bills. In addition, she owes $100,000 in taxes. If she paid that right now, she would be wiped out financially and have nothing."

"What's she going to do?" Ashley was instantly wrapped up in Jennifer's dilemma. "Where does she turn for help?"

"The first thing she's feeling is desperate," said AO. "Her circumstances are dire. If she only dwells on the problem, it could get worse."

Brian quickly offered a possibility. "Remember what William of Occam just told us—that sounds weird, doesn't it, that *he just told us,* since he died six hundred years ago—anyway, he said that the simplest path could illuminate the underlying principle to follow. Could she do that? Would that help her?"

"It could help her a great deal," replied AO.

"Then we've got to tell her," exclaimed Ashley excitedly. "You've got to help us tell her! How do we do that if she can't see us?"

"I'm afraid you can't do anything for her right now," said AO simply. "What happened to Jennifer McColm twelve years ago has already happened. You can't tell her anything at this moment. You can't disrupt the past except in your thoughts, and it is only there that someone's scars can turn into stars. This moment that you are seeing was up to Jennifer to decide. She had not met William of Occam as you have, but she intuitively sensed the truth concerning the underlying principle that would help her move forward."

"What underlying principle could help her out of this mess?" Ashley clearly wanted to know. "She doesn't even know where to start, does she? I mean, you said she doesn't have any idea of what kind of job to try that would give her enough money!"

"There were a lot of things she didn't know," said AO. "And she could've spent a lot of time ruminating about all that confusion. But she chose to look at things differently. She was desperate and clearly felt the fear that arises when you feel desperate, but she didn't stay at that place in thought."

"Where did she go?" wondered Ashley.

"She had a desire to move away from the problem. Creation arises from desire. That desire made her aware that a solution existed that matched her situation. *Awareness* of an existing solution was the first building block in the foundation of the underlying principle she needed to follow."

"That *awareness* came from within, didn't it? She didn't need to go anywhere to get it, did she?" Brian asked.

"That's right, Brian, very good." AO was pleased with the progress of Brian's thought process. "She was alert and open to ideas because terrible trouble had woken up every fiber of her being in order to be ready for change, ready for the change of thought that would reveal a solution."

"What were the other building blocks?" Ashley was anxious to know if Jennifer was going to be all right.

"Awareness is being ready for change. Once you have awareness, take action. Do not hesitate; be bold and the path will open before you."

"That sounds like something we should remember," said Ashley.

"Yes," answered AO, "that's a very good one. And this is exactly how Jennifer began her journey. She had three children, going to three different schools because of their ages, and this took up much of her time. At first, this seemed to be part of the problem—not enough time to deal with getting and doing a good job. However,

Jennifer realized that *you'll do more for others than you will for yourself.*"

Ashley and Brian heard one of her children call and Jennifer returned inside her house. Ash and Bri peeked in the window and saw that her children were all younger than they were—one girl was eight, another girl was five, and there was a little baby boy. Jennifer began preparing breakfast.

"This action of doing for others," AO continued, "will actually pull you out of your problems. It accelerates things so much more. She certainly wasn't going to forget about her kids, so she automatically knew they were part of the solution and not a problem. That was a key decision for her, one that would change her life."

"Yet she still had to deal with her kids." Brian felt as if this was still a problem. "I know I'm a real handful. I've heard my mom say that. So I guess this was a real problem for Jennifer."

"Yes, she did have to deal with her kids," responded AO. "And it meant she had less time for a solution."

"That's a rather limiting way to think about it, isn't it?" asked Ashley.

"With unlimited possibilities, there are no limitations. This means that a perfect solution exists for your particular circumstance—*if* you're aware—*if* you're ready for change—and *if* you don't stop its arrival by believing that it's not possible."

"I'll bet that wasn't Jennifer's only problem," guessed Brian.

"Jennifer did not have the financial resources to fund a company but she did have ideas. **She kept asking herself,** *What can I do?* Sometimes she was surprised by the ideas that came to her. She began compiling file folders for each potential project."

Jennifer paused in preparing breakfast in her kitchen and walked into her dining room, where the table was covered with file folders spread across its surface. Each folder contained ideas and notes for a potential project. She made a quick note in one of the folders and returned to her children.

"One project was a bathing suit to lift up your behind," said AO.

"Oh, my mom would buy a ton of those," offered Brian.

"I wouldn't let her hear you say that if you ever want to eat at home again," offered Ashley.

AO knew exactly where Brian's thoughts were running. "Would you like to see the bathing suit project?" Brian nodded enthusiastically.

They swiftly found themselves in the crowded workshop area of a seamstress, who was seated in front of a sewing machine. Patterns for the bathing suit design were laid out in pieces on a long table as Jennifer studied them. There were boxes of fabric and racks of clothes, but no other people except for Brian, Ashley and AO.

"Are the models getting dressed in the back?" asked Brian with healthy anticipation.

"There aren't any models," said Ashley knowingly.

"Why not? If she wants to sell this bathing suit, she needs *Victoria's Secret* models to help her," Brian said with assurance. "That's what I'd do."

"She doesn't have the money to hire *Victoria's Secret* models, silly. Can't you see how worried she is?" Ashley glanced at Jennifer, who tried different shapes of pattern without success. "She's not even done, nothing's working yet. She's still trying to figure it all out."

"But she's got to make this work!" Brian was trying to be encouraging.

AO smiled to himself and continued. "Another clothing project was something like Spanx, the support hose for women, and this was before Spanx came out. She tried a number of ideas, working up prototypes with the help of a seamstress. She was thinking, *Maybe I could do this*, or *Maybe I can do that*. There was a folder for real estate, and she looked into taking classes to get her real estate license. She designed a program to teach acting classes. Another folder contained ideas for setting up a day care business. She listened to people, alert to the possibilities. Her days were an expression of heightened alertness."

"Did any of these ideas go forward?" wondered Ashley.

"No, they didn't," said AO. "She didn't know what to do, but she did know what she wanted, the type of job she needed. There were three key things that came to her that acted as a guide. She needed something that didn't require a lot of money to start, because she didn't have a lot of money. It had to be something that didn't require a lot of time, because she needed to care for her children. And she wanted and felt she needed something that made money while she slept."

"That sounds like a whole slew of problems to me." Brian was a little confused. "Wasn't she boxing herself in and limiting her choices by placing all these problems in front of her?"

"Think carefully about what I'm going to tell you," AO said. "Intuitively she looked at this whole situation differently. In her heart, she knew she would find a solution because she *had* to, for her kids. It was something she didn't plan out intellectually; she merely walked in the direction of a solution. The key thing is this: *She took her problems of no money and no time, and instead of looking at them as a problem, she made them an element of the solution.* Dealing with those situations had to be part of the solution. This opened the door for the right solution to walk right in. She was already alert, so hopefully she'd recognize it when it arrived."

Brian was gazing at the bikini top for one of the bathing suit designs and AO realized it would be a good time for forward progress. "Let's go for a little walk," he said.

Instantly, they were strolling among the fruit, vegetable and food stands of a farmers' market in Calabasas, California. People milled about, buying items from the farmers who had brought their products directly to the marketplace from their fields. Most of the farmers offered organic products.

"Oh, look," cried Ashley, "there's Jennifer."

In the crowd, Jennifer McColm strolled among the stalls, carrying a bamboo shopping bag.

"Is this now, is this our present time?" asked Ashley. "Can I go up and say hello? I want to find out what happened to her and if she's okay."

"No, I'm afraid you can't do that yet," said AO. "This shopping day happened twelve years ago, just a short time after our day with the bathing suit design. But this turned out to be a very significant day for Jennifer."

"Did she meet someone?" wondered Ashley, suddenly excited. "Maybe a rich guy?"

"Maybe she went to pick fruit for one of the farmers," offered Brian.

"What happened next," AO said, "was something that many people laughed at. They told her she was crazy, that it would never work and she was wasting her time. And if you remember, Jennifer McColm had little time to waste."

AO didn't say another word. Ashley and Brian watched with anticipation as Jennifer picked out some kale and arugula. They waited breathlessly for Jennifer's *miracle* to happen, but nothing happened ... other than more shopping. Suddenly Jennifer stopped ... staring into her shopping bag, then gazing across the entire length of the farmers' market. In her eyes, something did happen.

"She sees something, doesn't she?" Ashley was excited.

"Or someone," stated Brian, following Jennifer's gaze. "But who is it?"

"Experience and its resultant insight await you," said AO.

Ashley and Brian were eager to know what this would reveal about Jennifer. They could hardly stand it and wanted AO to speak faster. Jennifer was still staring across the farmers' market, and

Ashley and Brian searched anxiously to understand what—or who —she was looking at.

"Yet not here," AO continued, "not now. For *now*, we must be somewhere else for you to fully understand."

"What!" they exclaimed simultaneously, and rambled on, their words spilling into each other: "What about Jennifer? What's she looking at? Who does she see! What's going to happen to her? We can't leave! We have to know—*now*!"

The last uttered **now** echoed all around them and Ashley and Brian found themselves underground beneath a city, standing on the edge of a sewer channel with churning water flowing like a river past them. It was dark. They were once again all alone. AO was nowhere to be seen.

Awareness is being ready for change.

Once you have awareness, take action. Do not hesitate, be bold and the path will open before you.

If one advances confidently in the direction of one's dreams, and endeavors to live the life which one has imagined, one will meet with success unexpected in common hours.
~Henry David Thoreau

CHAPTER SEVEN
The Solution Notion

7

THE SOLUTION NOTION

The concrete runoff channel was filled with rising, rushing water because up above, in the city, it was raining. If the water rose much further, Ashley and Brian would be swept away. There was nowhere else for them to go.

"This probably doesn't help us much at the moment," said Brian tentatively, "but I've heard there might be alligators in the city's drainage channels."

"Hello—hellooooo, hello— hellooooo." Tommy's voice echoed off the walls and around the corner to where Brian and Ashley clung to their little section of wall. A moment later he appeared around the corner, frantically paddling a rubber life raft filled with cats and dogs. "It's raining cats and dogs up there—and there are alligators in this water!"

Sure enough, a giant eighteen-foot alligator was swimming right behind Tommy's raft … and gaining rapidly. Tommy paddled faster but the alligator was closing the distance. The dogs and cats barked playfully at the alligator as if there was nothing wrong, but Tommy was petrified.

"I'll try to come back for you later!" yelled Tommy to Ashley and Brian as he paddled furiously around the next bend and disappeared.

The giant alligator swam right up to Ashley and Brian. With a humongous swish of his tail, he slammed to a stop right next to them and opened his gaping, powerful mouth, exposing rows of jagged teeth!

"Hi, you two, how'd you like to go for a ride?" The alligator winked at them. It was AO! His teeth sparkled like stars in the dark channel of swirling water. He propelled himself upward with his tail and twirled around in the water like a dancing dolphin, then settled next to the two kids. "Tommy thought I was going to eat him. He still isn't aware enough to see things differently. Hop on, this will be fun!"

Brian stepped aboard upon AO's scaly back and offered a hand to Ashley to help her climb on. They felt something attach to their feet and looked down to see that the rough scales had folded over their shoes to hold them in place and keep them from falling off.

"I am now going to show you how the big time adult world really works," AO said. "It has three basic aspects: money, power and influence. Money is Wall Street, power is Washington D.C., and Hollywood, the press and the entire media community are influence. Big corporations are part of all three. This system is the same everywhere, no matter what country you're in. For instance, in China, Shanghai equals Wall Street, Beijing equals Washington D.C. and Hong Kong is the media center."

AO swished his tail and they set off on a leisurely journey through the rain-swelled waters of the runoff channel. He was now a fully white alligator with large, glowing-pink eyes.

"We're under New York City right now. It has an almost endless labyrinth of rain runoff channels, sewers, subway tunnels, underground passageways, and well, it's almost like another world entirely. This is how we're going to get to Wall Street. It beats the midday traffic, that's for sure."

Up ahead, a swirling whirlpool sucked water down a large drain. AO calmly and easily swam past it. Ashley and Brian looked back and saw a wooden crate carried along by the rushing water get pulled toward the whirlpool. The box was marked *The Old Economic System* and was quickly sucked right down the drain. AO swam on without any concern whatsoever.

"I'll bet you want to know how Wall Street got its name," said AO. "Well, at one time the high, mighty, and powerful wanted to keep themselves segregated and away from the incoming immigrant peasant population, so they literally built a wall to separate who belonged and who did not. They wanted to keep the hoi polloi out. They are operating the same way again today; most people just don't recognize the schism. The rich and powerful have always desired to keep the poor out and to keep all the money for themselves. They had no desire to share the wealth, and practiced the art of the closed system. I'm scheduled to give a speech shortly at an important gathering that you will be attending, and I will show you how the new open system will transform our world."

"Is this a gathering of people?" asked Ashley.

"Yes, it is," said AO. He smiled because he knew what she was thinking. "I will not be attending in my current form. They're not quite as receptive as you and Brian are to my many expressions."

They passed by markings on the wall of the runoff channel that corresponded to the street above. It read: *Wall Street*.

"People on Wall Street and Main Street need to wake up and be more aware, if the system is to recover in a healthy way. The same people who caused or contributed to the crash are heavily involved in the current crisis correction."

Brian was not very comfortable with this. "Are they capable of crashing the system again?"

"Yes," said AO, "if the public fails to stay informed and connected to what is transpiring. The government and the media were duped by high-flying financial experts who spoke in terms so convoluted that few knew what they were talking about. Not wanting to appear out of touch, others who should have known better did not speak up and ask what was going on. There was a complete lack of a moral compass. As my great friend Edmund Burke, who was a member of the British Parliament, once said, '*All it takes for evil to succeed is for good men to do nothing.*' This is something for everyone to solve together. It is your responsibility and the responsibility of all others."

"And one of the easiest things to change, that doesn't require money, equipment, or lots of people, is your thinking," said Ashley.

"That's so right," agreed AO. "If you ask the right questions, the image of a solution develops, just like a photograph sitting in chemical developer liquid in a photographer's darkroom. Being in the dark can be good, if you let it be and don't try to force an answer, for it is there that the image of what you want to see can develop. These dark periods are not to be fought. Let go of any outlining as to how things *must be* and, like a cork bobbing to the surface when it is released underwater, you will naturally return to your receptive state of mind and a solution will develop."

"Well ..." pondered Brian. "One night I heard my dad ask my mom a frustrated question while they were discussing family finances. He said: *The stock market is fueled by greed and whipsawed by fear ... is this something we want to completely rely on with our investments?* That sounds like a good question to me."

"It is, Brian," said AO. "And it's one that might prompt some enterprising and free-thinking individual to create an exciting new solution. Continual unchecked greed will carve a path for one future. A radical re-imagining of your financial system will pave the way for another future."

AO swam over to the side of the runoff channel at a point where the walls were huge stone blocks, set in place more than a hundred years ago. He hauled his massive body out of the water onto a concrete shelf with Ashley and Brian still on his back.

"This may be a bit tricky," said AO. "I want you to sit down and hug your knees and duck your heads slightly, okay?"

The two kids sat down and complied with his request. As soon as they were comfortably tucked into position, AO's alligator body began to vibrate, then stretch and expand. It folded up around them, encasing them in an alligator-hide suitcase, complete with rollers and a telescoping hand grip.

The ground beneath the suitcase rippled and moved forward, acting like a conveyor belt as it tilted upward toward the street level. Just before the suitcase reached the top, a metal plate slid open and the suitcase rose out of the darkness of the runoff channel and was deposited in a storage room.

Everything was very quiet until the door to the storage room opened and a young man in a business suit entered, walking directly to the suitcase. He extended the telescoping handle and wheeled the suitcase out of the storage room.

The suitcase was wheeled down a busy hallway with people in business attire walking hurriedly in both directions on either side. A sharp turn brought the suitcase onto the stage of an indoor corporate amphitheater designed for large presentations. The young man left the suitcase behind the lectern. A crowd of four hundred business men and women took their seats.

The lights dimmed. The latch on the suitcase clicked open. The sides unfolded and inflated, lifting Ashley and Brian upward until the alligator hide formed into three chairs. The kids rested on two of the chairs and the third was empty. AO was missing again. The kids stared out at the crowd, who stared back at them with increasing curiosity and anticipation.

An announcement came over the speakers on the walls. "Ladies and gentlemen, welcome to our presentation."

Brian leaned over toward Ashley and whispered. "Are we supposed to present a speech on something?" The lectern was tall and loomed before them.

"I don't think I can reach the microphone," said Ashley.

The announcer's voice filled the amphitheater. "Let's give a warm round of applause to our guest speaker."

The audience clapped, their eyes glued to the stage. Brian shrugged his shoulders and started to stand when he noticed the empty chair next to him stretch upward. The chair re-shaped itself into a white Brioni suit that for a split second was empty and standing on its own. Then feet popped out of the legs and hands jutted from the sleeves and a head emerged from the collar. By now, it was not surprising to Brian that this was AO.

As AO strode to the lectern, a screen behind him filled with a PowerPoint banner that read: *Life Insurance Executives of America.*

"Gentle people of America and the world," began AO. "Ever feel the problem is too **BIG** ... and you're standing outside of it, waiting for someone else to solve it because you feel too **little**? Many great companies that now supply solutions for the world began in garages—Hewlett-Packard and Apple—or from dreamers with a grand vision—Microsoft and Virgin Records—or in a college dorm room—Facebook. People are now ready for change because of the impact of the current troubles. Everyone who is aware is conspiring, for the first time ever, to make the world work for 100 percent of humanity.

"Yet the world has entered the most severe economic depression in history. Wall Street has robbed America and the world of hope by absorbing all the money in the most unethical and devious of ways with derivatives, funds on funds, offshore title house accounts that are illegal, over-wrapped mortgage securities that were a hundred to a thousand times overvalued and sold through and by respectable houses and institutions that did not care what happened to the customer, all the time duping Washington power brokers with lies, deceit, and falsehoods. We are at the precipice of the greatest economic collapse in history, due to what could be thought of as the greatest heist in human history."

The kids were astounded to hear all this from the *Sage of Sages*, as they privately called AO. They realized, however, that he was using this speech as a tool to get the audience's attention.

"There are four economic engines that make America work: Wall Street and all its financial institutions—including what I will speak about immediately, the life insurance business; real estate both commercial and residential; banks; and the auto industry. When you change your direction, you automatically change your destination. Our current direction has us moving with accelerating acceleration toward disaster, a depression, and all kinds of expected and unexpected deprivations. Wrong thinking got us here, and if we continue, will keep us here.

"I want to offer some right thinking for right results, right now. I want us to agree in principle, spirit and fact to move forward together, starting today, to save America and the world both financially and factually, with life insurance as savior number one.

"When Social Security was invented and launched in 1937, it was supposed to be an insurance-like product, an insurance savings plan that guaranteed money when people needed it in old age, for the first time termed *retirement*. We copied Kaiser Wilhelm's program in Germany. At age sixty-five, a worker who had paid into the program received prescheduled benefit payments. *It was a safety net to supplement an individual's own personal and family savings.It was not meant to cover everything completely until death.*

"The fact is that when this program was established for the elderly and disabled, in case another Depression ever happened, life expectancy was 47 years of age; so basically, they never expected to pay off. Then two major things happened. One, politicians who thought they had a dollar to spend chose to spend twenty, mortgaging our kids' and grandkids' futures and finances. They took the Social Security nest egg and squandered it. And two, individuals decided that the goal was survive to 65 and to thrive on the government "dole and free lunch" program. People began to live longer and to cash in on their retirements, with the ignorant expectation that the government could fund their longevity and health care costs. None of which is true, then, now or ever.

"Soooo, that's where we have been and are ... The question is, where are we going and how can we get there? Social Security, welfare, universal health care and the like are noble ideals to be sure, though not well thought out, planned or designed to work effectively as they are currently structured.

"You all have it within your power to solve the problem. In fact, U R the Solution—individually and collectively—especially as we execute this plan.

"Life insurance works! Here is one simple application of life insurance realizing a debt-free, stress-free, set-free America and world once again. Imagine that this is only one piece of a seven-piece puzzle that we will consider. I want to make this easy to understand, easy to apply, and easy to do. The problem with its simplicity is that it's also easy *not* to do, easy *not* to apply, and easy to let slip by, which means an even bigger disaster looming.

"We will assume that we can come to agreement and make it happen. After all, you are the make-it-happen people. Slightly oversimplified, to balance and pay off the American national debt we need eleven trillion dollars. We can no longer 'off' our paper onto China, India, the Middle East or Europe. They are not buying it until we get our own house in order.

"Dr. R. Buckminster Fuller taught: RW = I x E, which is REAL WEALTH EQUALS IDEAS TIMES ENERGY. Theoretically, ideas are infinite, if the mind is programmed to believe, think, look for and act on solutions. According to the laws of thermodynamics, energy is *intracontrovertible* and cannot be exhausted, wasted, used up or destroyed; it simply goes through multiple transmutations. **Thus, we can infinitely expand REAL WEALTH with our thinking and awareness.** That's the general, macro, or deductive thinking.

"The specific point of application is this: Eleven trillion dollars means we need thirty thousand dollars for every living American. We can work this out for the world later, but the same principles apply. We create a life insurance policy for thirty thousand dollars per American. Each individual can either contribute a one-time, single premium payment of $365, or a dollar a day for a year.

"This money is put into a *Save America and Make it Debt Free* plan. Each American gets to deduct $730 from their taxes for the next year, after they have invested their full $365, as an incentive so that more people will do it. The thirty thousand dollars is granted to be paid exclusively into our Federal Reserve Bank upon each individual's death. It will take a while, perhaps fifty years, to pay off the national debt; yet, it is proof positive that we are doing something to make amends for our flagrant and excessive spending.

"Obviously, politicians must stop over-spending and spending what does not exist.

"You say this is preposterous; it can't be done, it has no precedent. Please know and come to understand that that's not true. When Senior Minister Lee took over Singapore as a benevolent despot fifty years ago, Singapore was the poorest, most uneducated, backwater country in the world. Today, only fifty years later, with a fifteen percent straight tax on every citizen, Singapore has the number one airline—Singapore Air; number one airport—Singapore International; number one sea port—Singapore Waterways; and the number two financial port in the world, behind Switzerland.

"Their population has risen from sampans to high-rise buildings. There are no bag people or poor people; everyone retires on a government pension of more than enough to live on because they pay 20percent of their income into a compulsory retirement plan. The people are educated, respected, happy and well-traveled. The roads are spacious, well-designed boulevards lined with flowers and glorious foliage year round. All this and much, much more because they had, and have, a fifty-year plan.

"America's plan is *What will I do for lunch*? We can and must have a plan—individually and collectively—starting today."

AO returned to his chair behind the lectern and sat down with Ashley and Brian. From the audience there was a smattering of applause, snippets of snickers, a cascade of chuckles, rolling dismissive laughter, waves of apathetic silence, and one lone burst of enthusiasm.

Ashley and Brian deeply wanted to make AO feel appreciated. They didn't like the overall response of the audience to AO's impassioned speech, but AO had no worries. He was beaming. The kids wondered if he hadn't heard the laughter or felt the vibes of derision that floated about the amphitheater. He gazed out at the dispersing crowd with a complete sense of love for all who had attended.

"***Big ideas***," AO began, "***no matter how crazy they may seem at first, have within them the seeds for a future harvest***. Big ideas should not be discarded even when people laugh at you for sounding preposterous. Big ideas get the engine of ingenuity revved up."

Ashley and Brian felt AO's supreme confidence glow around him like an energy field, attracting more light with every thought. They felt compelled to be within the warmth of this expression.

"Now's the time to hear the answers to the questions you had asked before, for now you will be receptive to the answers in a way that touches on understanding and not just curiosity. Are you willing to take another journey?"

Both kids nodded enthusiastically, and no sooner had they agreed than their chairs began to melt and they sank to the floor on the surface of the warm, soft gel that used to be their chairs. AO had actually melted into his chair and was no longer seen. The gel of all three chairs flowed together into one connected and cushioned environment.

The edges of the gel glowed green, then the colored light spread from the outer edges throughout the entire melted substance. As the light advanced, the gel crinkled and wrinkled and thinned out into a leafy texture. Both kids breathed deeply of a smell that was familiar to them. As the now-leafy blanket curled over them, cocooning them inside, they recognized the smell. They were being enfolded in kale and arugula leaves.

Their cocoon swayed gently back and forth as if they were in a hammock. They heard the rustling voices of people around them but could not make out the words. It seemed as if they were being carried. The forward movement stopped and the rocking motion gently settled into stillness.

"Are you ready to see what she was looking at?" AO's voice was soft and gentle and all around them.

"AO, where are you?" asked Ashley.

"You've been in my arms all along," replied AO.

"You mean you're the kale and arugula?" Brian was flabbergasted.

"And why not?" replied AO. "If I'm everywhere, then everywhere is here."

"I'm ready," said Brian confidently. "I'm ready to see whoever's looking at something or whatever it was you asked if we're ready for," Brian added somewhat hesitantly.

"It's Jennifer McColm, isn't it?" Ashley knew this was true. She really wanted to know what or who Jennifer was looking at when she stopped and stared at the farmers' market. Ashley wanted to know what happened to her, if she was okay, if her kids would be okay.

"Yes," said AO, "it's Jennifer McColm." The kale and arugula cocoon of AO unwrapped around Ashley and Brian to reveal that they were resting in the bottom of Jennifer's bamboo shopping bag. They gazed up to the top of the bag and saw Jennifer's face turn as if in slow motion to look down at them.

"Watch carefully," alerted AO. "A big idea can come to an individual in the strangest places, for reasons they don't immediately understand, even if they have no clue how to make it happen."

Jennifer's face turned completely to look down in the shopping bag, and she was now staring right at … the kale and arugula. The light in her eyes traveled with recognition into her past and illuminated a memory of childhood.

"She's staring right at us," exclaimed Brian, amazed.

"No, silly, she's staring at the kale and arugula," replied Ashley. "Not everything's about you."

"Well, Brian's not entirely wrong this time, and you are also right, Ashley." AO continued as Jennifer's expression filled with a thought that began in memory and bloomed in wonder to the hope of a possibility. "She's looking at the kale and arugula, but she's also looking back at her childhood, which you two represent right now, so you have helped her with this recognition."

"What *about* her childhood?" Ashley was deeply interested. She could see the smile in Jennifer's eyes as the idea she was embracing took hold in her thoughts. It was clear that it came from her heart, for it felt true to her.

"When Jennifer was a little girl, other kids set up lemonade stands to make a little money. She was a little different. She had her own organic garden, so she set up a stand to sell organic strawberries and other organic produce."

A simple warm smile of inner delight lighted on Jennifer's lips and her eyes twinkled with the spark of creation.

"You see that smile, that glimmer in her eye?" asked AO. "That belongs to everyone; it is always there for everyone to be able to feel that. You see, and this is important to remember, *the big idea comes because it has been invited by one's awareness and desire and joy-in-spirit.*"

Jennifer lifted her gaze from inside the shopping bag and stared across the farmers' market in a state of deep contemplation.

"Is she looking at anyone or anything now?" asked Brian excitedly.

In the next instant, as if in response to his question, Brian and Ashley stood at the other end of the farmers' market with AO at their side, now dressed in the t-shirt, jeans and straw hat of an organic farmer. Jennifer was staring right at all of them.

"She's staring right at us," said Brian.

"No, look carefully," Ashley implored. "She's not looking at anything or anyone. She's deep in thought. I think she's looking into her heart."

"You're very perceptive, Ashley," remarked AO. "You can see in her eyes that the idea is settling in, finding a home, and the spark of possibility has ignited the fire of desire. Right now you can see she knows what she wants to do. Wanting is a first step. Will she follow the leadings of her heart? The next step is determined by whether someone believes in it enough and is bold enough to act on it, despite the naysayers."

Change yourself and you change the world.

---

*The big idea comes because it has been
invited by one's awareness and
desire and joy-in-spirit.*

CHAPTER EIGHT
The Solution Called You

8

THE SOLUTION CALLED YOU

Ashley and Brian both had binoculars and were looking through them where AO had just told them to focus. They didn't know it, but these were not ordinary binoculars; they were **Binoculars of Belief.** Through the magnified lenses, both kids saw hands digging in the dirt. They were a woman's hands, loosening the soil with a trowel, then spreading it around the base of a small lemon tree in a large ceramic pot. The area had been cleared of weeds. Then two little girls' hands brought in small watering pitchers and emptied them onto the soil, soaking the planting area. Brian and Ashley both tilted up the binoculars and saw Jennifer McColm and her young daughters.

"What are you guys looking at?" Tommy walked up behind them.

When they turned to look at Tommy, they discovered they were no longer at the farmers' market—and AO was no longer there. And "there" was a hillside, looking down into Jennifer's backyard.

"We're looking at Jennifer McColm plant a lemon tree," said Ashley.

"We asked AO what to do when you're trying to get a business started or find a job," said Brian. "And he told us to do what you should do all the time, which is **_do what you love, because it's all connected_**."

"And then he gave us these binoculars," continued Ashley. "But when we looked through them we were no longer at the farmers' market, we were here, and she was planting this tree with her daughters."

"Who on God's green earth is Jennifer McColm and what were you doing at a farmers' market?" Tommy was annoyed and feeling slighted. "You missed most of my radio broadcast, and it was a doozy! I skewered everyone. Everybody was yelling at each other by the time I went off the air. It was great."

"That's real helpful," said Ashley. "If you wanted to do something good, you'd get interested in helping Jennifer. She's divorced and desperate to find a job or start a business so she can take care of her kids."

"She just came up with an idea at the farmers' market and we don't know yet what it is. We thought when we looked through these binoculars we were going to see what it was she wants to do, but all we saw was this tree."

Tommy took Brian's binoculars and looked at Jennifer's lemon tree. "That's a really scrawny tree. Why's she wasting her time with that?" Tommy gave the binoculars back to Brian.

"She's doing what she loves," said Ashley assuredly. "She had an organic garden as a little girl 'cause she likes to plant things."

"Isn't that just randy dandy," said Tommy. "That's gonna make a HUGE difference in her life, just _monumental_." Tommy thoroughly enjoyed his facetious humor. "Wait a minute—McColm, Jennifer—yeah, I know her," Tommy realized, and began to laugh. "This is just another stupid thing she's doing. I know what her *great idea* is too—what she thinks is going to work." Tommy laughed even harder now. "You're wasting your time with her. It's not going to get you any closer to home. All you're going to do is watch her fall on her face, because she doesn't know what she's doing. The idea she wants to do, which is really a reach, especially for someone who doesn't have a business degree, is something that she doesn't know anything about." He walked off without waiting for them to follow.

"Where are you going?" asked Brian.

"To get some lunch. Watching this woman try to do this *great idea* of hers is like watching a train wreck. It'll just give me indigestion."

Tommy disappeared over the hill ... and the kids silently stared at each other, wondering if AO wanted them to see what Jennifer was doing so that they would learn what *not* to do. But they really liked Jennifer, though they had not really met her. She was nice and pretty and fun, and seeing her made them both miss their moms.

Finally, Brian said, "How come everybody knows what Jennifer's *great idea* is except us?"

"You'll know it when you believe it like Jennifer does—in your heart," said AO, who was once again standing right beside the kids. For some reason he declined to divulge, he was dressed as a swashbuckling pirate with a bandanna around his head, a blue sash across his chest holding a glistening cutlass at his side, and a blazing white parrot on his shoulder.

"I'll let you in on a little secret," whispered AO. "That lemon tree is going to save her entire idea, the new business she wants to launch."

The blazing white parrot piped up into the conversation. "He's right, you know. That lemon tree will save her."

"Thank you, Fernando," said AO. "You don't always have to agree with me."

"Yes, I do," said Fernando. "I have to parrot whatever you say. It's what I do. I'm a parrot."

"All right, but use proper parrot paraphrase proficiently this time. And say hello to Ashley and Brian."

"Ahoy, mateys," squawked Fernando.

"Ahoy," replied Ashley. "AO, is Jennifer going to fall on her face with her idea? Tommy laughed at what she wants to do."

"That's what Tommy believes," said AO. "What you believe is where you direct yourself. It's also where you determine whether you can or can't do something. You accept your belief and your belief creates *you*. Remember, you are the sculptor of your life. Playfully re-imagining yourself as the solution opens up a space where awareness, powered by focus, creates a new *you* that is fully present and results-generating."

"Playfully re-imagine," chimed in Fernando.

"Do you think Jennifer should let Tommy's laughter stop her from moving forward?" asked AO.

"No, not if she believes in what she's doing," Brian stated positively.

"What if she has no guarantee of success before she starts?"

"I think if she feels right about it, she should go ahead anyway," said Ashley. "You told us: Don't swim in the problem. Sail toward the solution."

"Set sail, hoist the main mast, avast you swabs, clear the decks," barked Fernando. "Now you're talking! Shanghaied aboard another adventure with the Crimson Pirate!"

"Fernando," said AO patiently, "do you have anything important to say?"

Fernando flapped his wings like a drum roll, took a deep breath, and rolled the following words off his tongue and past his beak until they hung in the air. Each word lit up one by one and Fernando's voice echoed the sound. "*Being bold is moving forward without a guarantee of success.*"

"Jennifer was bold," said AO. "Nothing was going to deter her. Not laughter, not doubts, not even lack of knowledge. And what she wanted to do was indeed something she didn't really know how to do, but she felt that she *could* do it, that she would figure it out, because the idea felt right."

"Did she start a lemon tree grove?" wondered Ashley. "Organic lemons?"

"No," said AO. "However, that tree will play a big part in her success."

"A really big part," Fernando paraphrased proficiently.

"Jennifer McColm decided she could put together a farmers' market herself, even though at the time she didn't know much about them except that she liked going to them. With the solution in mind, visualizing an established market, she began walking in that direction."

"How'd she do that? She didn't have any instruction manual," said Brian.

"Ah, but she did," said AO. "The same instruction manual everyone has, the one you're born with. It's your intuition, your gut feeling, your goose bumps; all of those come directly from your heart. Many people laugh at this because they think you only get instruction manuals at Harvard or Yale or Stanford or some other smarty-pants place. They literally stop themselves from doing the very thing they want to do because they feel they don't know enough. They lack a conscious sense of self-worth and feel that someone else has to give it to them, either from a book or in a class."

"Books and class are good for you, aren't they?" Brian was perplexed.

"Yes, of course they are," said AO, "as long as they are not your boundaries. If they are launching pads, that's great. If they are limit lines, they're not."

"I want to know all about Jennifer," said Ashley. "Does being a pirate have anything to do with her plan?"

"I'm a possibility pirate, reminding you to be bold in your solutions. You must learn how to discern the truth, no matter what clothes it's wearing. Would you believe me more if I wore a business suit? Perhaps you would believe me too much, too readily, without doing your own thinking. What is true, is true, and you must know it when you *feel it*, for your eyes can easily deceive you. Tommy laughed at Jennifer because she doesn't look like what he thinks a creator of a farmers' market business should look like."

Ashley and Brian were becoming more aware that AO's many ways were not just because he was eccentric, but because he was alerting them to an inner truth, to the way things really were, and to a better way of thinking.

"Now pay close attention to Jennifer's story. It is **not** just her story. It is not simply and only the story of one California girl and her problems. Pay attention to Jennifer's thought process and the principles behind her actions. These can work for you in wanting to go home, and for anyone, whatever they want to create or do. This is why I'm showing you her journey. It has universal significance and can benefit everyone."

A small pirate ship floated by and stopped next to them. Her sails billowed in the wind. No one was at the helm. The ship rocked gently on the energy waves of this glorious day.

"Oh, here's our ride," said AO cheerily.

Ashley and Brian stepped aboard, followed by AO. Fernando flew up and settled in the crow's nest, which he quickly renamed *Parrot's Perch*. AO stretched forth his hand and the sails snapped taut, driven by the *Winds of Wisdom*. The ship floated effortlessly over Jennifer's backyard.

"From this higher perspective, we can get above the problem and see the solution more clearly," said AO. "This is exactly what Jennifer did with her thinking, although we might be having a teensy, weensy bit more fun in our pirate ship. Our conveyance is simply a reminder that you should embrace *fun* each day."

Leaning over the port side, Ashley and Brian gazed down at Jennifer. She made notes on a writing pad while resting in the sun near her lemon tree. The task before her—setting up a farmers' market—seemed complicated and a waste of time to many others, but Jennifer was energized by the challenge and the vision she held of her goal. A gust of *Wisdom Wind* filled the sails again and the pirate ship floated off, banking right, on a course for Calabasas, California.

On the stern, the name of the ship was emblazoned in golden light on the wood panels above the Captain's cabin: ***Tertium Quid***, and in smaller letters underneath: ***of the Agape Argosy.*** Sailing on the *Air of Authority*, the pirate ship approached a bank of billowing clouds. The bowsprit extending off the prow was the trident of Neptune adorned in garlands. Just as the trident cut into the cloud bank, Fernando swooped down from the *Parrot's Perch* and landed on its tip.

"Hard aport!" called out Fernando. "Rudder amidships," he squawked. "Steady as she goes," he bellowed as his feathers ruffled in the wind.

The ship cut a path along the rolling edges of the clouds like a surfer carving a line in the waves. Ashley and Brian reached out and grabbed glistening globs of clouds in their hands. They molded them into perfectly round spheres and began a cloud-ball fight with them. Laughing with delight, they pelted each other with the misty puffballs.

They were thoroughly engulfed in rolling mounds of cute cumulus. When the *Tertium Quid* burst through the thick cloud bank back into crystalline blue sky, a seagull suddenly barrel-rolled out of the eastern sky and shot straight across the mizzenmast, raising one wing in salute as he passed.

"Ahoy, Jonathan," AO called out. "Great to see you again! Have fun!"

As if acknowledging the loving command, the seagull rolled over on his back and floated past them one more time. His wings rippled the air generating waves of music and filling the sky with the notes of Beethoven's *Ode to Joy*. As the last note vibrated along the gunwale of the vessel, Jonathan gave a final nod, then in the twinkling of an eye, he was instantly and delightfully somewhere else.

Fernando lifted effortlessly from the trident bowsprit and flew back to the *Parrot's Perch*, somersaulting to a perfect landing as if to say that the seagull wasn't the only one who could put on an aerial acrobatic display. Ashley and Brian clapped enthusiastically which uplifted his spirits. He puffed up his chest and proudly gazed forward—then squawked, "Land ho—off the starboard bow!"

The *Tertium Quid* dropped a feather anchor to hold it steady in the breeze above the Calabasas farmers' market. Down below, Ashley and Brian saw Jennifer McColm in conversation with a group of vendors as most of the market participants began packing up their product.

With confidence and determination, she had gathered the farmers together and told them of her plan to open a farmers' market in her canyon community of 600 homes. At first, Ashley and Brian could tell that the farmers were skeptical of this pretty young blond woman weaving her tale of a new venture. Why should they leave the market that was already up and running to shift their loyalty to someone who was untested?

Jennifer did not let their doubts faze her. She approached this as if she was putting on a play and gathering her players and stage crew. She had taken only a smattering of business classes in college, nothing that would have prepared her for this undertaking. She had been a theater major, a far cry from a business degree. But she had put on plays and felt that this could be like putting on a production. The same principles applied. Her approach was honest and sincere.

Something about her directness and enthusiasm intrigued the farmers, and the rest gathered around her after packing up their products, to hear more of what she had to say. Her confidence created an aura of comfort for the vendors and soon they were open to her suggestions.

All this happened despite the fact that Jennifer knew she had no working knowledge of how to establish a farmers' market. She was merely following the vision of the market she desired. A significant part of that desire was for this market to be profitable for both her and the farmers. This inclusive and unselfish principle was her guide.

Ashley and Brian learned by listening that good business could benefit all concerned. Jennifer knew that most farmers' market organizations, like this one in Calabasas, charged the farmers a flat fee whether or not they sold anything. In a slow market, with few customers, the farmers were out of pocket the same hefty fee no matter what. The organization always profited, but the farmers did not. They only made money on a good day of selling. If it was raining and few people came, they still had to pay the full flat fee.

Instead of a flat fee, Jennifer offered them the opportunity, at her soon to be farmers' market, to pay a percentage of their profit, which meant that the farmers did not have to pay anything unless they sold something. She proposed that they pay only a small percentage and keep the remaining profit. With this simple idea, Jennifer found the underlying principle that William of Occam had told the kids about: to include everyone in the expression of good. This idea gave the farmers great flexibility in their business.

However, none of the business people Jennifer knew liked her business model. They counseled against instigating her percentage payment plan. Their fear was that the farmers would cheat, as there was no way of knowing whether they were paying the percentage based on their total sales. That number was too easy to fudge and hide.

Jennifer was not naïve to the temptations besetting human nature. She knew that some farmers might cheat—and some did—but reasoned that this might allow their business to start and thrive. When they did prosper, thus getting beyond their fear of failure, their natural tendency toward honesty returned and most properly reported their correct earnings. More importantly, the farmers knew from her actions that she was with them and not just in it for the money. In the long run this engendered loyalty, and the farmers stayed with her through tough times. Her farmers' market business survived when others went belly up because the farmers stuck it out with her.

Ashley and Brian had been absorbing everything as they watched the proceedings unfold. They knew that AO allowed them to hear and feel everything through some sort of spiritual osmosis. Suddenly Ashley realized there was a missing piece to the puzzle of how Jennifer pulled it all off.

"What happened with the lemon tree?" inquired Ashley. "How did that save her business?"

"Remember I told you to do what you love?"

Both kids nodded.

"Well, Jennifer planted that tree out of the love, for the simple joy of doing it, before she even knew she wanted to start a farmers' market business. When she set up her business, she used her own innate intelligence to guide her toward her vision, but she was ignorant of all the official steps that should normally be followed. Some of that ignorance allowed her to cut corners with more efficient ways of getting started. From that she learned a very good lesson. Do you know what it was?"

"That you don't have to know everything to do something," said Brian assuredly.

"That's right," replied AO. "Self-doubt will get you to believe you must learn it all first. There's a wonderful saying from one of my favorite people. His name is Ray Bradbury and he is one of the very best writers and storytellers to ever grace your planet." AO smiled from the sheer pleasure of telling the kids about Ray Bradbury.

"When faced with a challenge, standing at the *Cliff of Risk*, Ray is fond of saying that you should *jump off and build your wings on the way down.* I so love his joyous spirit of adventure and his deep trust in the goodness and guidance of love. If you ever want to curl up with a good read, grab one of Ray Bradbury's books and be prepared to tingle with delight from your hair to your toes as you wrap yourself in the blanket of his words and wander down the story path he has carved out of the *What If Woods* that he has planted before you."

"That's what Jennifer did, didn't she?" asked Ashley knowingly. "She did what Ray said. She took a leap of faith and built her wings on the way down."

"Yes, indeed, she certainly did," said AO. "Once Jennifer convinced the farmers to come join her new market, she got everything set up to receive them. However, she was not fully aware that the state mandated you must meet one of three requirements to be able to legally organize a farmers' market. You must either be a non-profit organization or government agency or a certified farmer. Jennifer didn't qualify for the first two and she had no idea what you needed to be a certified farmer."

"Oh no," realized Brian. "You said the farmers had already left their old market and were coming over to her new set-up. If the state shut her down before she even got started, the farmers would never come back."

"That's right," acknowledged AO. "They would never trust her again. So just before she had to show proof of qualification, Jennifer called an official who certified farmers. She asked him what she needed to do to be a certified farmer. He, in turn, asked her what she had in her backyard in the way of plants. She replied that she had a lemon tree in a pot. He then verified that she had a lemon tree in a pot, sitting right in her backyard. Then by the powers vested in him under the law, he dubbed her a certified farmer, thus qualifying her to establish a farmers' market."

"And did everything go wonderfully after that?" asked Ashley expectantly.

"Oh no, not at all," said AO. "There were challenges left and right, up and down, day and night. One of the very first problems that arose threatened to erupt into mutiny among the farmers. She brought in more than one vendor to sell strawberries and more than one to sell flowers. The fear of competition spread like wild-fire and many of the farmers were up in arms that there wouldn't be enough money to go around."

"Weren't they right?" asked Brian. "I mean, why did she do that? Did she know it would make them upset?"

"Jennifer knew this decision was based on a solid principle of abundance. Most people look at business as a pie. They feel there are only so many pieces to go around and you must assiduously protect your pieces from the competition. Jennifer never saw the pie as not having enough pieces for everyone. She felt that if she added more people selling strawberries and more people with flowers, having more choices would encourage more customers to come to the market. There would then be more money spent and more opportunity to increase their profit. In essence, this means the pie gets bigger. It keeps expanding. It's not limited."

"With this thought," realized Ashley, "you feel better about working with others and there's less fear. Everyone can feel free to thrive."

"And you can be much more profitable working synergistically with others than you can all by yourself. This is the power of community. Jennifer understood that in her heart. She didn't have to read it in a business textbook."

"Does she still have the farmers' market?" Brian wondered hopefully.

"Yes, and seventeen more," said AO. "Jennifer McColm now runs what's considered the largest independent organization of farmers' markets in southern California. And she's branched into other businesses, creating a company that certifies organic and 'green' businesses and products with a label the consumer can trust. She has written a book on healthy living, developed her own line of organic products and is developing a television series on healthy living. Her website, www.jennifermccolm.com, is evidence of joy in the journey."

"The same joy she had as a little girl when planting an organic garden," said Ashley, realizing the limitless possibilities for her own dreams.

"Jennifer believes that the energy that is creative is like when you were a little kid on Santa's knee. There was no limit to what you wanted. You asked for the moon and beyond. Your creative choices were on fire. That gets doused when people push that childlike energy down with all the ways they believe it won't work out, until finally you stop asking. Jennifer knows that the little child in all of us is liberating and powerful. Perhaps this is why your Bible states that *'a little child shall lead them.'*"

The clouds rolled across the sky above the *Tertium Quid* forming letters as they passed: ***The solution begins with realizing and believing that U R the solution.***

"Take with you some lessons from Jennifer's story as we continue our journey," said AO. "Realize that on a deeper level, thought and action are one. If thought is wrong, then action won't be right. To think only of yourself and your own gain is shortsighted, but many don't think of it that way. They think it's smart to get it all for yourself. That's the underlying premise and one of the pillars of greed, the belief that it's a closed system and there's not enough for everyone. When fear dictates your steps and you don't walk in faith, you live in lack and limitation and will have a lackluster experience no matter how much you have. However, faith and the expectation of good allow you to see, feel, express and experience the abundance that is your true spiritual nature. When you get beyond ego to true wisdom, you will understand this more clearly."

"Why don't we see the whole picture of abundance all the time?" asked Ashley. She clearly felt in her heart that what AO had said was true. Yet it seemed a feeling that was fleeting at times ... too many times.

"What you are really asking," said AO, "is *How do we see this spiritual perfection that always is and always was?* Humanly, you see it as progress, sometimes in little steps, sometimes in leaps and bounds, sometimes a glimpse of uplifting light, sometimes a warm feeling in your heart. And it expresses itself in more and more good in your experience, until all that was bad no longer has a fear grip on our thought or a presence in your life. You then see the bad for what it always was, merely a suggestion to be believed. It was nothing more than an invitation to believe that the world is flat."

The *Winds of Wisdom* once again filled the sails of *Tertium Quid* and the pirate vessel weighed its feather anchor and set sail for parts unknown. The trident bowsprit poked through the thin veneer of the blue sky and a black hole into space opened up before them. As they sailed beyond the *Event Horizon,* they descended past the point from which light can no longer escape. Ashley and Brian were not afraid, not at all. They felt the tingling excitement of Einstein's words: *The most beautiful experience we can have is the mysterious.*

Conscious sense of self-worth is not given to
you by the opinions of others, but is embedded
in your heart by God and can't be taken away.

The only real valuable thing is intuition.
~Albert Einstein.

R U vibrating at the frequency of
the problem or the solution?

CHAPTER NINE
URS Synergy

9

URS SYNERGY

Tingling anticipation surged through both Ashley and Brian. Though they saw nothing around them in the haunting, ethereal blackness, something was building ... something was coming closer ... something that felt explosively powerful.

AO stood steadfastly at the helm of the *Tertium Quid*, undisturbed in the vast, deepening darkness. The kids drew courage and inspiration from his almost droll, dreamlike demeanor, for he was calmly decisive and definite in his actions. The way he steered the ship created the feeling of floating, not on flights of fancy, but rather on the flow of fortitude.

It was then that Ashley and Brian realized more fully that something wasn't coming closer, *they were being pulled to it,* along with particles of matter and waves of energy that were drawn inexorably forward with them. Brian recognized a gathering of familiar elements in this ever-deepening black hole, something he remembered from physics and astronomy.

"Wow," said Brian with elated anticipation, "we're in a black hole being drawn toward *the singularity*, aren't we?"

"A certain type of *singularity*, yes," said AO.

"What's *the singularity*?" asked Ashley, who wouldn't have that class until next year.

"It's this really cool place," Brian began, "where everything that gets sucked into a black hole—light, matter, energy—gets compressed down into such a tiny smashed amount that it's actually infinitely dense—and you know what's really cool? Time stops at this place."

Ashley turned to AO with just the slightest hint of concern. "Are we going to be smashed into something really tiny? I guess it might be okay if it doesn't really hurt and we get to spring back at some point, but if we don't, how will I fit into my clothes when I get back home?"

AO smiled warmly, delighting in her resiliency in the face of *believed* imminent calamitous change. "Your clothes will all fit, there will be no fashion felony committed here. This is a black hole of a different kind. You will learn later what leading quantum physicists are discovering and what I've been telling everyone all along, that your universe is constructed of consciousness, not particles of matter. What you see around you are particles of belief and energy waves of thought, which will soon explode into the light of understanding. This is exciting, Brian, because what you are experiencing are the moments before creation, the coalescence of thought into a *singularity*."

Suddenly, all motion stopped. There was activity all around them but it was circular, going nowhere. Particles swirled and waves traveled in endlessly repeating loops. The only light came from the lamps on board the ship, and the light they cast bent into curved rays at the gunwales and returned back onto the ship.

"Are we here?" asked Brian. "Is this *the singularity*?"

"I don't feel squished," said Ashley, relieved. She thought for a moment, taking in everything around her. "We're in a swirling negative vortex, but we're not moving, we're not going anywhere."

And indeed, they were not. All movement had stopped. They were stuck on dead center. They were in a state of complete thought and action torpor.

"Depression is from non-circulation and isolationism," said AO. "Nothing happens. Remember I told you that my good friend, Albert Einstein, said '*Nothing happens until something moves*'? That is the nature of your universe. While we *seem to be stuck here* on dead center, let's look around."

Ashley and Brian looked ... staring at nothing ... and it felt familiar.

"You both sense that this is what your society looks like right now," said AO. "Fear has become pervasive and the result is a tourniquet on money. No one can move or know, with any kind of assurance, when to move. If a tourniquet on the arm is too tight, the arm eventually becomes gangrenous and falls off. Many people still feel the problem is bigger than them, that the people or systems dealing with them are bigger than they are. They need a new concept of possibilities and of people working together. The actions in your financial world knocked out trust with a shocking collapse, leaving only a whirlwind of fear, and doubt and distrust are tightening like a tourniquet."

Ashley and Brian both remembered the stunned and frightened looks on the faces of their parents as *everything had changed for the worst.*

"What you—and your society—are experiencing is that circulation stopped. Banks are holding onto the money and not lending for fear they will run out, businesses are holding onto their money and not hiring, consumers are holding onto their money and not buying, people are staying home and not connecting, then becoming scared and lonely as a result of their separation.

What happens to your body with no movement, no exercise? The body becomes sludgy and you slow down, then eventually you stop, unable to move altogether. An error in the premise—believing that holding onto your money will keep you safe—leads to an error in conclusion, and instead of progress you find stoppage. You must get your thoughts moving forward, or your economy and world—and you—will be on dead center forever."

"People are praying for answers. That's good, isn't it?" Brian was hopeful.

"There's an old proverb from your continent of Africa that says *'When you pray, move your feet.'* It is a reminder that thought and actions are one."

"But how do you move when you are sick?" wondered Ashley.

"In your Judeo-Christian Bible is an answer," said AO. "Jesus said many times to the incapacitated and sick, *Take up thy bed and walk.* It was a command to move your life and thought forward, away from the image and belief of yourself as sick, and this action of movement was tied to the understanding that your real spiritual nature is eternal health. Your world, environment, and economy suffer under *the belief* that they are sick. It needs to move, based on the right uplifted premise—for life is movement. To deactivate the problem you've got to activate the solution and move in that direction."

"I heard some of my parents' friends talk about that in an odd sort of way," added Ashley. "They thought if everything was so bad that it was all going to end, they wanted to activate their *bucket list*, all the things they wanted to do before they die. They said *the heck with it*, we're going to travel and see the world. They wanted to have fun without fear."

"Well, they are certainly right about one thing," said AO. "Fun without fear generates enthusiasm for life. Enthusiasm wakes up the awareness of infinite possibilities. With infinite possibilities, life is always in motion. With that in mind, here's another **Big Idea**

Game Changer that few people see ... the seven-trillion-dollar travel industry. If everyone took one more trip, the economy would snap back into motion. One of the reasons this could work is that it would break the magnetic pull of fear that keeps everyone locked on dead center. If many people decided to do something positive and fun—without worry—and take a trip, the thoughts of many others would conclude that tough times were lifting and they'd want to get moving again. *If you want to be free, you must first feel free in your heart. To be prosperous, you must move forward with a prosperous attitude.*"

"Well, let's go then!" said Ashley excitedly, without hesitation.

"Yeah," agreed Brian. "Let's rock and roll!"

Those thoughts suddenly shot the *Tertium Quid* forward in a burst of pure, blazingly brilliant white light and they came out of the black hole propelled by the *Big Bang of Creation*. It was an explosion within consciousness of thought so vivid that a new form manifested into view instantaneously. Up ahead they saw a natural series of reefs arrayed perfectly to provide clear passage through an inlet to a protected harbor. They anchored just off shore at a small but empty port.

Along with AO, the kids climbed into the *Dinghy of Delight*. Fernando grabbed a rope in his beak that was attached to the *Winch of Wonder* and lowered the dinghy over the side to the water below.

"I'm going to stay behind," Fernando squawked. "I'll swab the decks, trim the sails, stow the gear, and polish the brass bell, along with anything else my little bird brain can conjure up. You all go and have fun and don't worry about me!"

They rowed effortlessly to shore with pure white feather oars and docked at the wooden pier. A road at the end of the pier led into an empty town. A creaky metal sign swung in the chill wind. The letters on the sign were carved blocks of wood that hung from nails and rocked back and forth, side-to-side in the breeze. The letters read: *Welcome to rospero*. There was an empty space before the letter *r,* as if someone had misjudged when nailing the letters up on the sign.

"Where is everyone?" Brian wondered as he looked around at the empty stores and restaurants. There were no cars either. Blown by the wind, leaves scraped along the vacant pavement. It was the only movement anywhere. The place seemed completely abandoned.

"Are they all asleep?" Ashley glanced up at the sun's position in the sky. It was almost overhead, close to high noon.

"Send out a sonar ping from your heart," said AO. "The bounce back from the echolocation will tell you what you really want to know."

Ashley never doubted that she could do that. Instead, she closed her eyes and felt a pure and happy sense of wanting to connect with the people in the town. An energy wave sprang from her chest and rolled across town, a *sonar ping* echoing between the buildings.

A moment later, an echolocation sound wave bounced back toward them with a harmonizing *sonar ping.* To their amazement, there were words riding along the crests and troughs of the sound wave. As the wave passed by they heard the words as a feeling in their hearts, as if from their own voices.

> *One mind awake can awaken another,*
> *The second awake can awaken their next-door brother.*
> *Three awake can awaken the town,*
> *By turning the whole place upside down.*
> *Many awake can make such a fuss*
> *That they can finally awaken the rest of us.*

"That was really trippy," said Brian.

"Poets speak to the heart," said AO. "Those words were from a poem by my friend Helen Kromer, a wonderful writer and poet— and just what you needed to hear, so you'll know what to do.

Their footsteps brought them to City Hall, where they heard the rumble of voices from a town hall meeting. This is obviously where all the people had gone. The kids were relieved to discover that *rospero* is not a ghost town after all. However, the more they listened, the more the rumbling voices sounded like arguments and insults hurled back and forth. They considered that maybe they should skip this meeting.

"If you are afraid, don't go in," said AO simply. "But if you are hopeful, you can be a catalyst for change. What you hear inside is not just nasty noise. Things are shifting, arising out of the big trouble in the world. There is a moral chemicalization underway, a stirring up of thought, and because of it, a readiness for change. Everyone who is aware is conspiring to make the world work for 100 percent of humanity."

"That could really mushroom into something great!" exclaimed Ashley.

"It's already happening," replied AO. "Evidence of this action has already been around you in nature from the beginning. You are in the swells of a *Fibonacci sequence* of thought and action. In nature and mathematics, this is a sequence that repeats, but repeats bigger. In mathematics it is a sequence of numbers that expand, spiraling upward. It is also a mathematical pattern of progressive expansion expressed in nature, from the tiniest of structures such as the strands of DNA and the patterns in which capillaries are formed, to the spiral array of sunflower seeds and all the way up to the spiral patterns of the stars in the largest galaxies.

"In the universe of consciousness, the spiraling effect of thought in the collective consciousness of the world can move nations. Fundamental within this concept is that one person or one thought can grow and have a tremendous global effect."

"Where does such a big thing start?" wondered Ashley, feeling slightly overwhelmed and insignificant in the face of that definition.

AO's response grounded her in assurance. "One person in alignment has more power than one million out of alignment. In 1988,
The Journal of Conflict Resolution published a study known as "The
International Peace Project in the Middle East." It revealed startling results from an experiment during the war between Israel and
Lebanon that had begun in 1982. A group of people used transcendental meditation to achieve the feeling of peace within themselves
during specifically assigned times. During these active periods, the
rates of crime, violence and accidents measurably decreased. The
statistics of the results were so accurate, they were able to determine a mathematical formula for how many people it took to effect
change in a larger group. The number was surprisingly small. Like a
Fibonacci sequence, the more people involved, the faster the effect
is felt."

"Wow, I'd like to be part of something like that," replied Brian
hopefully.

"You can be—every day," said AO. "You can initiate something
like that with your own thought, by yourself, and you can do wonders. Then, if you like, you can go further and discover the *third
new mind.*

"The *third new mind*? What's that?" Ashley had never heard of
this.

"It's the thinking that arises in the spirit of cooperative harmony
among two or more people working together. This third new mind
operates on the force of synergy. Two or more people working in
the spirit of cooperative harmony and pursuing one or more goals
form a synergetic *third new mind* that is invincible and unstoppable."

"Yeah, but it's not always easy to get people to cooperate in harmony," bemoaned Brian.

"Cooperation is natural when you know that the universe operates at the level of connection. Individuals can do makeovers
quickly, though systems cannot. However, if enough individuals do

it, the system changes over automatically." AO saw a glimmer of expectation in the kids' eyes. "Do you want to see how it works?"

"Oh yeah!" they both replied.

Within the blink of an eye, the city hall doors blew open and they walked into the town hall meeting of *rospero*. But instead of harmony, they found a hundred of the town's citizenry arguing about the awful economy and their respective plights in it. Activity within the town had stopped.

"I can't get a loan; our friendly banker is no longer friendly, considerate, cooperative, kind, or willing to lend me money for more fast-growing, delicious and nutritious dwarf money-making apple trees for my tree farm," spewed farmer John McApple.

Henry De Nied, the banker, defensively responded. "I can't lend you money, just because you THINK these new dwarf apple trees will become the sixth fastest-growing privately held business in America. I don't know if they would grow in *rospero*!"

"'Anyone can count the seeds in an apple, but only God can count the apples in a seed' is ancient farm wisdom," chimed McApple. "I have always had a green thumb, have one now, and can help get my *green* going if you will stop with the constipated thinking that is immobilizing our growth. Johnny Appleseed was a nurseryman, like me, and invested forty-nine years of his life in the wilderness, foresting America with apple trees from Massachusetts to Illinois, because he believed he could.

"Even before the Beatles sang about it, he got a little help from his friends. Pioneers, Indians, and wild animals were his constant companions. Johnny planted trees for everyone and told them to eat the apples and save ten percent of the seeds for him. He promised to return and pick them up each season and continue his traveling to re-forest this new land called America with edible, life-generating, ecology-benefiting trees. Why, he was a 'tree hugger' before it became popular and the *in thing* to do."

AO, hearing everyone complain and sing the *ain't it awful* songs, brought out slices of *Possibility Pasta*. He wore a freshly pressed Italian waiter's outfit and spoke with a jovial, flamboyantly rhythmic Italian accent.

"Eat this pasta, special pasta. It has the magnificent effect of changing positive ionization, which is negative to life and has been charging through the air here. Everybody in southern California knows that when the Santa Ana winds blow, the positive ionization makes people crazy. This pasta transmutes positive ionization into negative—which is actually positive, like the good feeling you have in a shower. You know how you love to sing in the shower! So here, now, eat, mangia, mangia, enjoy and be happy after that painful, gut-wrenching, mind-debilitating debate."

At the first bite, the townsfolk's attitudes began to morph and change from depressed, despondent, disconsolate, angry and filled with angst to open-mindedness, joy, conviviality, possibility-thinking and seeing that maybe, just maybe, something could make their town successful again, and make it and the world work once more.

The first to speak to each other, surprisingly, were Henry De Nied and John McApple. Henry felt that his bank could advance enough to get John started with his apple business; apples were healthy and people always wanted to be healthy, so they would always buy apples. Ruth Cooksome immediately said she would place an order from McApple for the pies she wanted to bake; people always wanted pie, either to eat or to have pie fights with, which could be really fun. Daniel Diner was out of pies for his res-taurant, so he sat down with Ruth to discuss a deal, because people always wanted to get out of the house and eat somewhere else.

"These new attitudes draw more good into your experience," AO addressed the entire crowd. "While your awareness awakens, let me entice you with another tasty morsel. Travel is the awareness expander. Travel broadens and *inculturates*—how's that for a nifty new word?—*inculturates* you by plugging you into and through other cultures. The goal is to become world citizens and to inspire the same in others. The vitally important thing you share with others is that you all inhabit this small planet—and that simple fact makes you important to each other."

The possibilities dawned on the townsfolk, one by one. Ashley and Brian served up more heaping helpings of *Possibility Pasta* as AO continued.

"Imagine if you will, travel ... the biggest non-military industry in the world, which banks more than seven trillion dollars per year. As the world relies less on petrochemicals and moves to solar, tidal, wind and geothermal income energies, the price per barrel of oil will plummet and the economy will rock again. Oil has been as low as ten cents a barrel and as high as $147 a barrel. As demand decreases, it will go back down to $30 a barrel ... and travel will double in a year, to fourteen trillion. This will help synergize the get-up-and-go of our economy. Almost everyone has a dream to travel on their to-do 'bucket list'. Exotic and exciting lands around the globe beckon one and all! This will also help to get you off your collective keesters and get moving."

Thoughts of an active life danced in the heads of the assemblage. They felt a rekindling of hope and remembered what it was like to be action-oriented.

"Desire, arising from principle, ignites vision," said AO. "From the light of that vision comes ideas. From ideas, people gather. Then you can set priorities for which steps to take first in order to manifest the vision. When you turn to your Divine Source for guidance, advisors will come, in whatever form you need them."

Just then, ten-year-old Wendell McSignage burst through the front door.

"Guess what I just found?" Wendell was quite excited. "This fell off our town sign when the economy crashed." Wendell held up a

large carved block of wood in the shape of the letter *P*. "We were all
so afraid, we forgot the name of our town. It's actually *Prospero*!"

Ann Nouncer rushed into the town meeting, out of breath and
so excited that she almost put a dent in Wendell McSignage. "I've
got something to tell you all!" Ann Nouncer said breathlessly. "All
the people from *Usville* just arrived. They decided to take a trip for
fun without fear, and they're all outside. We have so much work
servicing their needs and wants that we won't even have time to
count all the money we're going to make!"

A crescendo chorus of cheers rose from the crowd. The mayor, a
very pleased and plump Paul A. Tission, realized that if he could
convince the people of *Usville* to stay, he could be the mayor of
the new town named *Prosperousville*! This was pleasing indeed.

Paul A. Tission stood atop a box of *Sudsy Sales* soap bars and
proclaimed, "Let the joyous news be spread! We at last will be
rolling in bread!" As the celebrations began, AO and the kids
walked back to the dock.

"You've seen something very important here today," said AO.
"A sculptor sees what no one else sees. A sculptor looks at a faulted
piece of marble and sees the *David*. Individuals connected by inspiration meet their solutions in the solitude of their souls. From
there, they reach out to us all. However, we are a communal species, and it is when we work together in synergy that global greatness appears. *Everyone who sculpts their solution, in synergy
with others, creates 'the' solution.*"

Ashley and Brian were happy to see the joy felt by everyone,
everywhere. Their own joy halted, however, when they saw that the
Tertium Quid had weighed anchor and sailed away.

"What happened?" wondered Brian, as he looked all over for the
pirate ship.

"I thought we could sail home on *Tertium Quid*," said Ashley.
"What do we do now?"

A little note floated down from the sky that read: *I had to go south for the winter. Nothing personal, it's just what I do. I retrofitted the Dinghy of Delight. It's fully charged and ready to go. Much Love, Fernando.*

"What does Fernando mean by fully charged?" asked Brian.

The kids noticed that the ***Dinghy of Delight*** looked decidedly different. Sleek like a bullet, it now was encased in a translucent polymer compound. The feather oars were gone, replaced by an energy orb that glowed bright green.

"Fernando said it was ready to go," mentioned Ashley. "Go where?"

"Exactly where it was designed to go," said AO. "The future."

What if 100 million people woke up every morning and believed in infinite good?

If you knew that infinite good was everywhere, you would fearlessly take the first step.

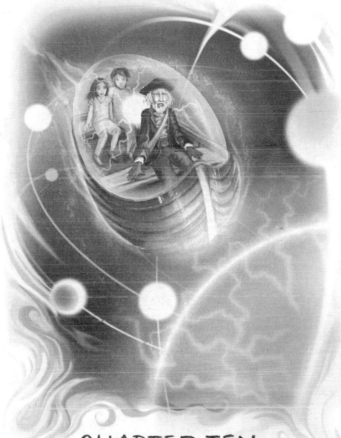

CHAPTER TEN
This or That...or Something Else

10

THIS OR THAT... OR SOMETHING ELSE

Strapped into the *Dinghy of Delight,* newly christened by Brian as the **Future FUNicular** because it took them *up, up and away,* the kids watched in awe as they soared through an array of colors like the aurora borealis. As usual, AO wanted their thoughts prepared before arrival, in order to take full advantage of the possibilities. They listened attentively as each of his words carried them further forward.

"Get your *Passports of Possibility* out before we get there," AO said. "We're going deep into the heart of the Imagination and you don't want them stopping you at the border for *limited thinking.*"

Not being restricted in how to think about things freed their thoughts and connected their hearts to the joy of creation. It felt like playing in the fields of Love without a care in the world. They were receptive. They were ready.

"*What if* you take a Godly point of view?" With that invitation, AO began to forge a possibility path for their thoughts "Get above the problem, not to fifty thousand feet, but a hundred thousand feet, or look back from a thousand years from now. How did the folks in your time actually solve the problem?"

This thinking was trippy, thought the kids. They were more attuned to AO's thought process now, able to surf those mental impulse waves like maneuvering a longboard at Surfrider Beach in Malibu. Their minds danced with new understandings. They were attuned to their current reality and the problems of their time, but searching for what a solution would look like in the future, where these problems had been solved without limitations.

"It isn't hard to imagine this," said AO, as if he was reading their thoughts—and of course he was doing just that. "You can make it real right now, for what you believe is where you direct yourself."

The colors outside the *Future FUNicular* intensified and Ashley and Brian's thoughts expanded exponentially. Images of future buildings powered by wind-driven energy, cars that used solar power and hovered off the ground to get past traffic problems, clean water drinking fountains that pulled water from the air, a world where poverty was only on display in museums, all these and more imprinted their inner vision.

"Looking at things from the perspective of the future stretches your imagination for what may be possible now," AO continued. "Remember, Jules Verne imagined flight and undersea travel years before anyone built vehicles to do it, yet those people were inspired by what Jules Verne imagined and expressed. If you can imagine it, someone, somewhere, sometime can build it. Maybe that someone is actually you. But you can't build an idea that hasn't been expressed, so don't hold back. Be playful with the use of *what if*. *What if* there was a way to pull water out of the air? *What if* there was a way to turn undrinkable ocean water into pure fresh water? Ask *What if* … and let your imagination soar."

Understanding filled them with great insight and the kids tingled with excitement. They knew they had latched onto a great freeing concept that could be put into immediate action, here, and back in the present. *When you are willing to* **LET GO** *and not outline how things must be, and simply align with your heart, this commitment allows the universe to open doors and bring the answers to you.*

As they looked out through the translucent polymer dome, the kids realized that their vehicle of the future actually was powered by the ultimate alternative energy—thought. It could bank, rise, dive and stop on a thought. AO was very pleased with their progress; they were realizing and seeing more of their true spiritual nature.

"Looking back from the future is a great way to open up your thinking, because it's not limited by the present problem. Dr. Buckminster Fuller taught this concept, to look back from fifty years in the future, because there is no political, economic or other expedient to stifle or stop your thinking. U R the creator of your future.

"It might surprise you to know that it's actually possible to look back from the future, according to the theories of leading-edge quantum physicists. According to their research and experiments, the universe is structured like a hologram, a 3-D projected image of laser light. For now, let me just say that every spot on a hologram is not just a little piece of the hologram, but contains every element of the whole hologram. Here's an example of how this works."

AO produced a glass water bottle by sculpting the air with his hands. He allowed the glass bottle to float in front of them, then used the touch of his fingernail to cut the bottle in half.

"If I had a bottle and I cut off the top, I would then have two pieces. One piece is the top half and the other is the bottom half. The bottom no longer has a top and the top no longer has a bottom—something's missing—and it's no longer a whole bottle. However, if I have a *hologram* of a bottle ... "

With a swirl of his hand, AO generated a 3-D laser light holo-gram of a bottle and floated it in front of them. This hologram looked exactly like the glass water bottle, but was made of light and was transparent.

"Now, if I cut a smaller piece off the top ... "

AO used his fingernail once more to slice through the laser light form about a third of the way down from the top. The surprising thing for Ashley and Brian was that the laser light hologram did not break apart. They were astonished at what they saw.

"Interesting, isn't it?" remarked AO. "As you see, the smaller piece is not just the top part of the bottle but an entire actual bottle, only smaller. And the other bottle is still a whole bottle, only not as large. No quality of either bottle is missing. That's because every single spot on the bottle contains all the information pattern of the whole bottle. Everything is connected. In fact, not only is every-thing connected to everything else, everything is everything else. The 'whole in every part' nature of a hologram means that nothing is disconnected or can be disconnected. Think of the implications of this."

Both Ashley and Brian pondered how this principle, this under-standing of life, had been expressed through time, even back to ancient civilizations. The Bible spoke of the oneness of being, of there being no separation from Divine Source, and that God is All. Native American Indians speak of the Great Spirit that animates the web of life, how everything is connected through this web, and what is done to one is done to all. This is why they honor the earth and its creatures as sacred, for they feel as one with them.

AO knew they were now ready for the next level of thought. "At the level of a super hologram—which is how quantum physicists say the universe is really structured—this same connection applies to space and time and reality. Everything is infinitely intercon-nected. That means that *over there* is connected to *right here,* and the *past* is connected to the *present* and the *future* simultaneously.

So it would be possible to connect with the past and talk with Benjamin Franklin or connect with the future and meet with his great, great, great, great, great, great, great, really great-grandson. Now *that's* really trippy."

Ashley and Brian recalled stories of famous people who had imagined the future and took steps toward making it real, right where they lived, then and now. Walt Disney was an *imagineer* way ahead of his time. He saw things that no one else saw. The important thing was that he did not hold back, he expressed those ideas —and look what he gave to everyone by doing that. The great storyteller, television producer and futurist, Gene Roddenberry, envisioned *Star Trek*. That world and its ideas stirred the minds of many to invent useful things for today, the popular Apple iPad being one of them.

"You are so right," said AO, slipstreaming onto their thoughts. "These are all individuals who thought they had a solution to the big problems of their time. **U have solutions that you haven't even thought about yet.** Remember, when the idea manifests, no matter how simple sounding it may be, capture and record it on paper with your Smart Pen, your video camera or whatever. Imagine fifty years from now. What could have happened? The auto business again boomed and got the economy rocking by melting down old gas guzzlers and converted them into EVs— Electric Vehicles—that charge in 37 seconds, do a hundred miles an hour in 4.2 seconds, are inexpensive and long lasting, and go a thousand miles per charge. Here's a little secret," AO whispered. "That's actually available in your present time. You may be seeing them soon from www.betterplace.com."

Ashley and Brian wondered for a moment where they might fit into this gathering of brilliance. For a split second, they thought they were inferior to these accomplishments, which were out of their grasp. Yet in the next split second, they knew what Walt Disney said was true for all: *"If you can dream it, you can do it."* The time between their doubts arriving and the moment of moving past them in the direction of a solution was quite short now. They were experiencing real progress.

"Ashley and Brian, you have never been more right," said AO happily. "What about solutions for individuals? Where would *you* like to be in your future? What is your passionate purpose in life? Are you running a business? Are you helping the community somehow? When you build backward from your solution, you will discover your beginning, which is where you are now, and you can then take your first step. Think of what you can accomplish with awareness powered by focus."

AO drew a square in the air and created a holographic TV screen. The onscreen image was footage of a pretty African woman with beautiful black skin receiving an award from the Secretary General of the United Nations. The entire assembly rose in a standing ovation. Tears of gratitude filled the eyes of every member of the audience as she accepted the award.

"You are watching a future that could be, that most assuredly *will* be, someday. This woman is Nia Makena of Kenya, or I should say Dr. Nia Makena. Her mother grew up in a poor village and had no chance of getting an education and improving her life, as a young girl. But someone helped arrange for a school to be built and maintained in her village. Nia's mother went to school … and it changed her life.

"When Nia was born, her mother raised her to believe that she could be anything she wanted to be, and Nia Makena became the first of her family line to graduate from college. That education and her drive to succeed, championed by her educated mother, gained her acceptance to Harvard Medical School. And today, many years later, the United Nations is presenting her with an award for finding a lasting cure for cancer."

"That's amazing!" said Ashley, thoroughly inspired by the efforts of this woman whose mother had lifted her out of an impoverished future. "How incredible would it be that the cure for cancer came from someone who got the gift of an education in a small African village, a place the rest of the world neglects to even think about. How did that school get built?"

"It was from the efforts of a woman from your present time," said AO. "Her name is Cynthia Kersey. She's an individual, just like you, Ashley. She wanted to do something that made a difference, that was a solution. The problem she saw was that 120 million children around the world do not have an opportunity for education and will not ever walk into a school. This holds them back. This holds their villages and communities back. This holds their country back. This holds back the world, for Cynthia knew in her heart that we all can't move forward when others are left behind. So she walked in the direction of the solution—building and maintaining those schools."

"Cynthia Kersey said it perfectly herself: '*The greatest natural resource in the world is not in the earth's waters or minerals, nor in the forests or grasslands. It is the spirit that resides in every unstoppable person. And the spirit of the individual benefits us all.*'"

"How is she doing all this?" asked Brian. "Can we help out?"

"Yes, you can," said AO. "Anyone and everyone can. Cynthia Kersey is an inspiration and there is a lot to learn from her. She is a great motivational speaker and the best-selling author of *UNSTOPPABLE* and *UNSTOPPABLE WOMEN*, two really great books that I urge you to read—they will change your life for the better."

Ashley was particularly interested because she wanted to learn what one woman, like herself, could do to be unstoppable in finding solutions.

"Cynthia didn't stop with just these accomplishments. She started the **Unstoppable Foundation**, which is building schools in Haiti and Kenya in 2010 and 2011 and beyond. Her goal is to educate at least 10,000 children in Kenya this year alone. The foundation raises money to build schools and to provide supplies, food, and everything needed to run the school and to keep the children in school. They have already uplifted and changed the lives of many children, thus securing a better future for them and their communities.

"When you see someone doing something wonderful for the world, you want to tell everyone—and that's why I'm letting you know about Cynthia Kersey. When you get home, go to www.unstoppablefoundation.org to learn more, and see what you can do to be part of this inspiring solution. It would be time well spent."

"The act of giving gets you great joy, doesn't it?" Ashley was excited to discover ways that she could give to others less fortunate, in gratitude for all that had been given to her. She knew how good it felt when someone believed in you enough to give you an opportunity to improve your life.

"Giving is an act of grace," said AO. "It enriches both the receiver and the giver. Cynthia Kersey refers to her campaign as *Give a little, Get a lot.*"

"I think I'm ready to dig into a good project," said Brian. "Can the **Future FUNicular** get us home?"

"It can, but I want you to be fully aware of the multidimensional thinking that leads to the most innovative solutions. For this we have to get right to the heart of the matter."

Traveling at the speed of thought, the **Future FUNicular** banked right and dove down through the radiant colors at a steep angle. The rushing colors blurred to a fine mist as their dynamic dinghy burst through a hole in the sky above a future city. Ashley and Brian glimpsed a gleaming metropolis with free-flowing traffic of electric vehicles, pristine parks, booming business, and no pollution, But only a glimpse!

Their vehicle approached the ground at high speed, and they didn't see how it was going to stop. Then they realized it *wasn't* going to stop! The closer to the ground their vehicle got, the smaller it got. They became so small that at ground level, they were rushing at a single granule of dirt. When they struck the dirt they had shrunk even smaller, penetrating the granule with ease and slipping inside an inner molecule, and then an atom inside that! But they didn't stop there—didn't even slow down—they sped right through the nucleus, dodging electrons along the way, into inner space!

Ashley and Brian were dumfounded. There seemed to be nothing here, nothing really visible. For a fleeting moment, they could notice a tiny particle when they looked at one spot long enough. But mostly they felt the caress of energy waves that they could not see.

"We are looking at the very building blocks of the universe," said AO.

Ashley and Brian squinted hard, but still didn't see anything of substance.

"Remember what I've told you," said AO. "If you want to really see what is there, you have to have a *MacGyver moment* and see it differently. Think differently. Newtonian Determinism posits a causal order to the world that says that *"this"* happens because *"that"* happened before it; and Aristotelian logic, with its many paths of *deduction*, guided collective thinking concerning solutions for centuries. Much of the world also thinks in a bivalent way— things are good or bad, on or off, right or wrong, this or that, a clear sense of either/or. This type of thinking sees the operating number of the universe as 2 rather than 1. For eons, this was thought to be the only true way to reason, the accepted way to chart a course through problems. But thought that seeks unlimited possibilities reaches for the **tertium quid** of life, **the third thing, the 'some-thing else'**."

"*Tertium quid*—just like the name of your pirate ship," exclaimed Brain.

"Yes, exactly," said AO. "It's a phrase in Latin, but it describes the state of thought I'm referring to, which is the deeper level you must be open to. For you, Ashley and you, Brian—or anyone else —what I'm about to tell you is like staring into the unknown and finding the courage to trust your heart, to listen to that *still small voice* inside. This might take a while to think about, but it will take you deeper in understanding your life. You are closer to home than you think."

That excited Ashley and Brian and riveted their attention.

"When you reach the *Cliff of Risk*, standing at the *Precipice of the Unknown*, truly being In-Spirit creates the inspiration that allows you to leap with faith ... and like Ray Bradbury says, *Build your wings on the way down* ... and then you soar."

The kids felt a tremendous energy all around them, yet still saw nothing.

"We are here, *in the heart of the matter*. Surrounding you are *quanta*, the subatomic building blocks of the universe that are nei-ther particles nor waves, but contain the essence of both. They are the threads of this magic carpet you call reality—a universe in which everything is infinitely interconnected—only truly under-stood in the depths of the heart. It's a leap of faith into a strange and startling world where matter breaks into smaller and smaller pieces until it literally possesses no dimension."

"If this is what we're made of, then where and what are we?" Ashley had never looked at it this way and now wondered about her identity.

AO did not answer her directly. "Subatomic particles are *some-thing* that are always both waves and particles, not just one or the other. This *something* you call *quanta*. And *quanta* are the *something* from which the universe is made. Yet the strangest phenomenon is that the only time *quanta* take the form of particles is when you look at them."

"That means," reasoned Brian. "That we actually give *quanta* its substance."

"It opens the door to an intriguing concept ... **that the substance of the universe is consciousness.** This is the new leading edge of quantum physics and an open door to what before was the territory only of the theologians."

"Wow, that would mean that we truly *are* what we think," said Ashley.

"Let me give you a practical example of this," replied AO. "In the mid-Eighties, your venerated Pulitzer Prize-winning newspaper, *The New York Times,* covered a story of a medical study involving patients with multiple personality disorder. Doctors made an astounding discovery during the course of this study. They observed one patient who had all the serious symptoms of diabetes and was being treated for it. However, when another personality took over the patient's consciousness, a personality who had no cognizance of having the disease, all symptoms vanished from the patient's body. When the primary personality returned to consciousness, so did the symptoms. Another patient had a scar from an accident. When a secondary personality took over who had no knowledge of this accident, the doctors watched the scar disappear only to reappear later, but not until the primary personality returned to the patient's thought.

"This startling discovery (and there have been many like this throughout history) reveals that thought indeed constructs our experience. ***Matter is objectified thought.*** This will certainly give you something to chew over. It should also alert you to how important it is to be in command of your thinking."

With the repercussions of this revelation rattling inside Ashley and Brian's thoughts, they felt displaced from how they had always believed everything functioned. But this ***tertium quid,*** this ***something else,*** was also liberating because they realized that they were in charge of their own thinking. It was up to them what suggestions to accept and believe. Is the world flat? Can man fly? Am I worthy? Can I find a solution to this problem? The answers were all up to them.

AO grabbed their attention back: "***A thinker's tools are questions***, questions you can use to probe for the solution. How do you see things differently, Brian?"

"Knowing there's no limit to how to see things differently is a good start."

"What is a good solution?"

Ashley answered. "Something that's as good for others as it is for you."

"How do you create a good solution?"

"You don't create it as much as you become *aware* of what's needed, and then walk in that direction, knowing that the solution's already there," said Brian confidently.

"You ask the questions to where the need most resides," added Ashley.

AO was delighted with the direction of their thoughts. He took them even further. "Thinking in the realm of **tertium quid**, you might even conclude that the collapse of your way of life is not necessarily a bad thing. Starting fresh, in a new direction and without baggage, is good and can have great advantages in the long run. The realm of the **something else** is a place that knows no fear, and without fear you are free to fly."

For the first time, Ashley and Brian glimpsed the power of unlimited possibilities and saw the open door awaiting them.

"The whole leverage of the world is U!" said AO emphatically. "Everything comes into U: media, problems, complaints, circumstances, situations, dilemmas, solutions and stories. U interpret it all and give it meaning, understanding, substance, and decide what to do about it, and you do something or nothing. It is all up to U. There are no real outside forces. U are in charge of U."

"Then the pathway home should be clear," said Ashley assuredly.

"It is," stated AO simply.

And it was. For when their thought instantly shifted to feelings about the home that they felt in their hearts, they were almost there. The nothingness inside the atom quickly manifested into a landscape they recognized. Ashley and Brian found themselves standing on the path of leaves where their journey had first begun. Before them, a short distance away, was the gaping hole through which they had plummeted.

The hole had now widened and split open so wide that the only way back was over it, for it was not possible to go around. It had expanded too wide to jump over. AO was once again nowhere to be seen. The only one they could see ... was Tommy, who stood on the other side of the gaping divide and signaled for them to come on over. He wore a welcoming smile. The only way home was past Tommy.

A thinker's tools are questions.

———

Being receptive is seeing with your heart.

———

Ideas are an infinite realm of possibilities and solutions are always around us.

CHAPTER ELEVEN
Soulutions

11

SOULUTIONS

Cumulus Nimble—The Wise Cloud Speaks

The situation facing Ashley and Brian was most challenging. This problem looked big—really BIG. The collapse of the ground before them had grown more expansive since they had fallen through a much smaller hole earlier in their journey. The gaping abyss was huge and there seemed no way around it without help. They definitely needed to get past the problem to go home. When Brian peered over the edge, his jaw dropped open and his knees wobbled.

"That is one scary deep pit," commented Brian.

"It's only scary if you intend on falling into it," replied Ashley.

"Not part of my solution, how about you?" Brian had regained his composure now that he wasn't gawking down into the endless spiraling darkness of the crevasse.

"Sure doesn't look like there's any way around it," Ashley said, scoping out the surrounding area.

"Yeah, it looks like we're pretty much trapped," agreed Brian.

"I think you guys are stuck over there," shouted Tommy. "You gotta wait for help and it may be a long time coming."

"Can *you* help us?" asked Ashley.

"I've been staring at this hole for quite some time now," said Tommy. "It just seems to get bigger. You might want to stay back from the edge before it collapses even more."

"What are you going to do for us?" asked Brian.

"Nothing I can do, it looks too big to handle to me." Tommy brightened up for a moment. "I thought of selling tickets to the *New Grand Canyon* but I think parking would be a problem so I nixed that idea."

"He's certainly not much help," said Brian to Ashley.

"Have you noticed he hasn't been much help since we met him?" Ashley already had turned her attention away from Tommy. "We've got to think differently about this. What would MacGyver do?"

Brian looked around. "Well I don't see any paper clips or duct tape, or much of anything really, except for dirt and grass and a few rocks."

Brian picked a rock and threw it into the deep void. He watched it fall into the gaping hole until it disappeared … and they heard a distant splash.

"Why did you do that?" asked Ashley.

"It was fun."

"Boys …" Ashley just shook her head.

"Well at least we know there's water down there," said Brian, extremely pleased with his discovery.

"Are we going swimming?" inquired Ashley pointedly.

"Ahhh … I guess not," admitted Brian.

"All right, then let's walk in the direction of the solution, because walking into the problem …" Ashley peered over the edge, "… is a long way down."

"Well, we're not afraid!" said Brian, striking a hero's pose with a big smile on his face. This made Ashley laugh—which made her feel better. "With no fear, we've cleared the playing field ... for play!"

"By watching, we are participators," said Ashley. "And we give substance to what we look at; so as we watch, we are aware, and awareness creates experience."

"Remember," Brian added, "Jesus said, '*What I say unto you, I say unto all. Watch.*' So we really need to watch our thinking, watch what we are accepting as reality." Brian now looked at the gaping pit of a problem in a new light.

Ashley was suddenly inspired with a thought. "If we start out holding in consciousness the understanding that everything is already all right, then we can go forth with faith and confidence, and see more evidence of what is always right here with each advancing step."

This inspired in Brian a recognition he felt instantly in his heart. "Original sin is the belief that you are separate from your Divine Source and must somehow struggle to get back home. Original innocence is awareness of what always is and always has been—the oneness of your being with all that is good. We always have our original innocence if our thought is open."

They were both on a roll now with their thinking, and slipping easily into the joy-in-spirit of the discovery of possibilities.

"Once you see the light of possibility," said Ashley, "it's yours forever; it never goes out, doesn't get tired, go on vacation, retire, or get scared. It only happily serves you—and darkness can't get near it."

Brian was excited by the idea that leaped into his consciousness. "Let's let go of how things should be and not outline. Let's get our thoughts in alignment with what we know to be really true and the path will open up."

"That's right," said Ashley. "Because conscious self-worth is not given to us by the opinions of others—or Tommy—but embedded in our heart by God. Our true lasting sense of worth comes from within, because we've always had it and it can't be taken away by anyone or anything."

Powerful feelings surged through both of them—feelings without words—an inner knowing. These vibrations were traveling at the speed of Love, vividly felt and explicitly real. With each wave of Love, a new energy of desire to be a catalyst for good flowed from them to all others. They were swept up in the joy of inspiration.

They were In-Spirit, and In-Spirit simply **IS**—it is *being*. They were willing to surrender the old picture of who they thought they were. They were willing to be "*born again*" of Spirit.

At this precise moment they heard AO's words in their hearts. "When what you perceive to be the end is near, do not despair from the depth of the darkness, for it is merely the grip of fear. It is but a shadow cast from a dream of sleep. When you wake, as surely you will, the light upon your face shall be from above and beneath. Thus, you will know that there is no spot where I am not. Never will you stand alone. From you I shall never part, for I am with you always, in your heart. Go forth into a brand new day, and the joy that is ever yours to feel will constantly and faithfully light your way."

Filled with this expectation of good, they moved confidently and powerfully forward—right toward the gaping maw of the endless abyss.

Tommy screamed and held up his arms to stop them. "No, go back, it's too big, you'll fall forever!"

Ashley and Brian both reached into their shirt pockets and pulled out the *Fear Free Glasses* that had been resting over their hearts. They slipped on the glasses and kept walking toward the edge of the seemingly endless dark abyss.

Tommy hurled one last warning of impending doom. "You can't do it, you're not good enough!"

Ashley and Brian both stopped at the very edge. They looked at Tommy and now saw him for what he really was—a belief—an illusion carved from fear. But at this moment, they felt no fear, and as they stared at Tommy ... he dissolved into the harmless mist from whence he came and floated off, whisked away by the currents of confident consciousness. Tommy was now what he always was—merely a *supposition*—and Ash and Bri no longer *supposed*, for they understood *that the world was not flat*.

Ashley and Brian stepped boldly and confidently forward, placing their feet right on top of the surface of the endless darkness ... and did not fall ... for the darkness was not there—only a solid path, bathed in the rays of a golden sun. Brian and Ashley were filled with the joy of understanding. They stepped happily forward, and the light of the truth that they now fully perceived filled their eyes with a bold, white-light brilliance, and ...

They awoke under the clouds on the hillside where they had first begun. It seemed as if they had never left. Comparing notes, they quickly discovered that they had shared the exact same vision and dream. Then they both heard the same thought: "**Look up from the problem; you are the solution.**"

Ashley and Brian scrambled to their feet. They were anxious to get home to put their solution into action, and they still marveled at the feeling that their whole wonderful adventure was a strange and exciting dream ... or was it?

Dotting the landscape were little patches of pure white ground fog. Ash and Bri passed by a knapsack-sized rock cocooned in fog like a caterpillar. As their feet shuffled by the cocoon, energy waves of joy broke the fog apart and it floated off in the shape of two white butterflies. Sitting on the rock for anyone to see were two pair of **Fear Free Glasses**, absolutely real and able to be picked up by hand or thought.

The kids happily continued on as they excitedly discussed their solutions without a scintilla of fear or doubt. Brian and Ashley spoke confidently as they strolled on toward home. Their vision was clear. The joy of awareness and discovery propelled their feet forward.

"Let's really think big and decide in favor of making a difference," exclaimed Brian.

Ashley jumped right in: "Let's make that a lasting, legacy generating difference."

They also knew that the entire journey didn't need to be taken all at once. They were confident that they could take the first step.

Giggling and laughing were their constant companions as they kicked around creative ideas for a website to wow the world. With their new energy, they wanted to inform the world of infinite possibilities that would create enlightened solutions, free from limited beliefs. Their website would be the gathering place for synergistic solutions to connect the world to infinite possibilities. Joy bubbled up and overflowed within them. The kids' enthusiasm and hope steamrolled over any and all negative thoughts that tried to sneak in and disrupt their playful creativity.

Ashley and Brian happily ran down the other side of the hill toward their homes, anxious to tell their parents all about their adventure. They would be home before they knew it, and in a very special way, they knew they were home already—the home they felt in their hearts.

Back on the grassy hillside, beneath a bank of white, puffy clouds, a man trudged along deep in thought. The blades of grass were still bent and folded where Ashley and Brian had stared up at the clouds, and in their innocence had heard the clouds talking. The man walked right through their impression on the grass without noticing, for his thoughts were troubled. He was beset with problems and saw no way out.

In his deepest despair, with his heart breaking, he had only enough strength to ask one question. He asked to be shown the way. He looked about ... and listened ... and was met only with silence.

Over the ridge, a woman gathering wildflowers in a small basket saw two pair of glasses resting on a rock. Bending down, she picked up the glasses and placed them in her basket. She looked around to see if anyone had left them, but there was no one in sight.

Closing her eyes, she listened ... listened deeply ... listened from her heart. She became very still with her breathing relaxed and her mind free from outlining. She was now very present with the moment. Then she heard the sound. It was the sound of running water, and it was very near. But when she opened her eyes, there was no water anywhere—near or far.

She trusted what she had heard. Doubt did not deter her. She knew there was water; she had heard it with her heart. Without hesitating, she followed the urge to put on a pair of the glasses, though she didn't need them. She raised the glasses to her eyes and looked through the lenses.

A smile of gratitude slid across her face, for the running water that she had heard was right at her feet. It flowed out from under the rock. It flowed down the hillside into the valley and it flowed up the hillside and over the crest. The babbling, gurgling rhythm of the water sounded to her like music ... and under the music were words. They were words she felt, not words she saw or heard, but felt in her soul, a place of original knowing.

"U R my pleasure, U R my joy, U R my soulution." Over and over the sound of the tumbling brook was the flowing rhythm of these words. The woman gazed at the water that ran up the hillside and felt compelled to follow.

As she crested the hill, she saw the man drop to his knees in deep despair. He had heard no answer, seen no sign, and had given up hope. Seeing him through the glasses, she saw something else entirely. She saw a man of great potential, bursting with ideas and the infinite possibilities of solutions.

She walked over to his side and intuitively rubbed the glasses clear over her heart before placing them in his hand. Her encouragement was all he needed. He lifted the glasses to his eyes and instantly his despair vanished. He saw the rushing, clear turquoise, heavenly healing water at his feet. It flowed in all directions. Wherever he looked there was abundance.

The woman took his hand and the sound of the water's rhythm was "*Go Forth and Prosper.*" With calm and confident steps, they stepped toward their future without doubts. They knew their purpose and their promise.

The sunlight glistened and glinted across the landscape, reflecting and refracting in dancing sparkles while leaping off the numerous glass lenses—lenses from *Fear Free Glasses*—an infinite supply as far as the eye could see. Glasses for everyone, everywhere, meant infinite, creative, exciting new dreams, aspirations and hopes, and a bigger, better, brighter future for all.

A magnificent and luminous white cloud hovered over their heads and followed them, acting as an ever-present guide. AO's whisper filled the sky: *"A Soulution is Source-Inspired and connects us to the infinite realm of possibilities."*

God always takes the simplest way.
–Albert Einstein

Being bold is moving forward without
a guarantee of success.

When you make a commitment to let
go of limitations, align with infinite
possibilities and not outline how it must
all work out, miracles will be real and
natural in your experience.

12

GO FORTH

Create, Find and Be the Soulution.

> *"We shall not cease from exploration*
> *And the end of all our exploring*
> *Will be to arrive where we started*
> *And know the place for the first time"*
> T.S. Eliot

U R about to drink in the final chapter of this story. Our fable is now yours; it has moved from the *land of never was and always will be* to reside in your **heart**. Now we want to validate the elements that make it real, timely, meaningful, and relatable to your life and future—complete with real-time solutions. The principles of the fable are pragmatic and practical and can connect with your daily human experience.

Everyone has a story, and everyone gets to re-create and rewrite their story. As storytellers, we deal in the power of ***What if ... ?!*** ***What if*** is the key to unlock and open the door to possibilities. We can change the stories we tell ourselves and others and thereby enlighten all of humanity. As Shakespeare wrote to *everyman*, we are writing to you—to inspire you to rewrite your story and make it infinitely better.

The ***AO adventure*** you have just taken is not merely fable; **it is the mindset** for creating your new and empowered reality. U can only solve problems when you are really looking for an answer; hence the Biblical line *"Seek and ye shall find."* There are answers and we are here to point you (and us) in some new and exciting directions. Some ideas are wildly outrageous and maybe even crazy, but ideas will stimulate you to create something better, wiser and more implementable. The practical examples you are about to see, and the proposed solutions we offer, all come from the mindset of unlimited possibilities. **When you think it, feel it, and envision it, you become it.**

Where you begin in thought is everything; how you continue in thought is everything. **Because mind is all and all is in mind**. The principles and integrity of your intuitive truth are the foundation from which your thought rises. The wisdom and truth espoused by AO is the awareness that awakens the solution within you.

We hope to be the gadfly that literally enlivens your spirit and excites you on the adventure of probing your imagination for new, innovative, original solutions. Solutions that are so omni-beneficial that they can serve everyone, everywhere, hurting no one and no thing.

We will start with an example of what one person with white-hot desire and determination did to overcome her challenges and create an economic miracle out of nothing. We believe that many of our beloved readers must now take nothing, ahh yes nothing but their own awareness, desire, and idea and turn it into something great and omni-profitable. And let ***no-thing*** stand in the way of your heart's desire and the service of all and to all. Examples of existing solutions from all over the world that are already in the works are provided as well.

Everyone sculpts their own life and story, whether they realize it or not. Be part of sculpting the solution individually, as we take part collectively. Man is an individual who lives in a community and culture. What that means is that we need each other. The great poet John Donne coined the phrase, *No man is an island*. Native American Indians have long spoken about the interconnected web of life, that no one stands alone or outside this web. We are all in this together and we want you to help us make it better in every good way.

Before you go forth, it is vital that your thought be aligned with your Divine Source and open to infinite possibilities.

We spoke of Jennifer McColm, beginning in chapter six, because we wanted to show that you can start with nothing, no particular business education or highly marketable skill, and yet, with awareness and against the odds, create and organize a profitable free enterprise—even in the worst economy ever. You will see, as you read on, that Dr. Hernando de Soto, the world renowned Peruvian economist, says to do exactly that, and we agree! **Give yourself permission to create an economic miracle for yourself and for everyone else!**

Take this to heart: It will always be the quantity and quality of products, services, and ideas, rendered with a positive mental attitude, that determines your eventual success.

Jennifer McColm's interest in green ecology and eating healthfully inspired her to start a local farmers' market that has expanded into what is considered the largest independent farmers' market organization in southern California, with a total of eighteen farmers' markets. She knew what she wanted to do, and inspired by Tony Robbins' tapes, took **two actionable steps daily to make her business move forward and make her dreams come true.**

She was desperate and divorced with three young children. She had inspirational desperation, and used her inner emotional guidance system to discover what to do next. Starting in Calabasas, California, in a canyon of 600 homes, she launched her business without first knowing all the proper steps. What she did know was that the limitations that initially seemed like problems that would hold her back actually needed to be part of her solution. She knew she needed a business that didn't require a lot of start-up money, because she didn't have it. She also knew she needed a business that didn't require a lot of time, because much of her time was spent caring for her children. And she wanted a business that would make money while she slept, so that she didn't have to always be there to produce profit.

Looking back, she realizes today that if she had had an MBA from a top business school at the time, she may never have taken the first step, because learned business experts thought she was crazy to take on this challenge. "*Sometimes,*" she has said, "*you have to unlearn certain things to free yourself and go forward, rediscovering the childlike energy and enthusiasm that knows no limits.*"

Because she courageously and bravely moved forward from a principle of inclusion, the farmers themselves helped her create a profitable organic farmers' market, which blessed her and them with profit. She understood that *the law of life is the law of growth,* and continues to expand her business into other exciting areas. She has launched an additional company, *Jennifer McColm Certified,* to certify farmers, vendors and green businesses as organic and ecologically sound. It is a service that provides *honest labeling,* helping the consumer to ascertain authentic organic and "green" products or companies. It's a label you can trust.

Jennifer has written a book on healthy living for publication and will sell her own product line of organic goods in major retail outlets. She is currently developing a TV show to bring healthful ideas to more people. To know more about her ongoing journey, visit her website: www.jennifermccolm.com.

You now know her story, the struggle and the triumph that resulted from thinking and acting toward the solution. Some people may think her success is a miracle, something beyond their grasp. Now you know better. It is something *supremely natural,* and those same expected, natural results can be yours. That is no miracle; it is simply the unfolding of Divine Love's plan for you.

You are walking forward looking at the solution not staring at the problem.

While everything in America and the world has become devalued in this recession cum depression, if we reinflate the human spirit, we can reinflate the economy. **What happens when one idea, even if expressed by just one person, changes everything?**

Everyone knew what everyone knew, and believed: *The poor were poor and would stay poor, because they were bad credit risks.* Leastways, that's what we all have heard, believed, and acted upon. Everyone somehow "knew" that the world's poor could not have credit, for a lot of *becauses*: because they wouldn't repay, they were illiterate, and how can anyone trust 'em because no one ever has, etc, etc... . until one man's thinking, desire, decision, and action changed everything.

Until Dr. Muhammad Yunus. Now 70 years of age, a Bangladeshi banker, economist and Nobel Peace Prize recipient in 2006, Dr. Yunus proved that the poor were worthy, honorable, trustworthy and paid back 98.7% faithfully—in full and on time.

During the famine of 1976, Yunus saw "the walking dead" in Chittagong, where he was a university professor. Yunus decided to do something. He found a lady making stools and selling them for twenty-five dollars, but personally earning only two cents a day. Yunus found that loan sharks were charging usurious interest and enslaving the poor. He personally launched the concept of *micro-credit* by lending twenty-seven dollars out of his own pocket to this woman and to 42 other women to help them get their businesses started.

To his amazement and everyone else's, all the women repaid the loans in full, with interest. Thus began a simple but revolutionary concept: Loan poor people money on terms that are suitable to them, and teach sound financial principles so they can achieve financial self-sufficiency, independence, and ultimately new levels of freedom.

Over the next six years Dr. Yunus struggled to create what today are called *micro-credit, micro-finance, micro-loans,* and *micro-business.* He launched the **Grameen Bank** in Bangladesh, which has become a nine-billion-dollar institution over three decades.

He learned a lot. Before he makes a loan, he has the women save two cents a day and bank it for a month; it teaches savings and gets them accustomed to being thrifty. The poor worked, earned, saved, repaid their loans, and encouraged others to join the program of financial self-sufficiency. Yunus teaches a woman or a man to learn to fish for themselves and thus be fed for a lifetime. Yunus wants everyone to be self-fed and a societal contributor. If we only feed a woman or a man, we create dependency and need.

Ask yourself: How many citizens of the world who have money follow this savings-mentality intelligence and ultimately profitable behavior? How many are practicing and teaching financial self-sufficiency, so that there is more than enough for everyone?

There is much that these impoverished women can teach the world. One thing for sure, they will not be impoverished for too much longer. *Can everyone else say the same about their own finances?*

When asked what he does that is different, Dr. Yunus says, "Whatever banks do, I do the opposite. Banks lend to men, I primarily lend to women (98%). Unlike banks, I'm not concerned with a borrower's past, but with their future. Banks are in the city, I operate rurally. Banks need collateral, I require no collateral. Banks require that you go to them, my staff goes fearlessly to the people."

Historically, we have always had poverty and it has become our prevailing belief. Any thought that you repetitively think becomes your belief and practice. **That belief in poverty, and that there must be poor people, is obsolete and outdated. The new model is that everyone can learn, earn, and return to help others**. There is fundamental abundance. *Yunus thinks that having credit is a fundamental human right.* With training and a team to support you, you are unstoppable and omni-beneficial.

Bravely, Yunus has shown that the poor have soul, heart, head, and ability when inspired and given a chance, guidance, encouragement, and the requisite instruction to succeed and prosper. Yunus's vision and Grameen Bank have helped a hundred million women rise from poverty and become economic contributors. They literally bloom where they are planted and are now able to feed, clothe and educate themselves and their family. He has proven that everyone **knows enough *now*** to start earning money today, once given credit and put in a team of five like-minded women who want to raise themselves by their own metaphorical bootstraps.

Everyone has a solution. **Everyone *is* their own solution.** Everyone can create a small enterprise, achieve self-sufficiency, and have it grow, develop, expand, and prosper. Everyone can become self-sufficient, a taxpayer, and an employer.

This proves that the old model, with the majority of taxes levied on the top five percent of income earners, is obsolete and antiquated. Everyone is coming to see the opportunities, harvest them, improve their stature and status and thus eradicate the financial caste system and end the plight of poverty.

Yunus says, "*The only place poverty belongs is in a museum*."

When Dr. Yunus first offered help to finance women's businesses, they rejected his offer, saying, "Give it to my husband." Women were afraid to accept the loans because of disruption to their family, their religious connections, and their husband's attitudes. Yunus persisted because he knew Bengali women handled the money at home and paid for the food, education and health care of their children. They needed to create money independently and consistently to truly care for their families on a sustainable basis.

Yunus wanted everyone to understand the simple, sound financial principles of buying or making something that can be **sold at a daily profit** and the value of a savings account the women had under their personal control, independent of their husbands. The conservative clergy rebelled against this, because it struck at the heart of their power and control in this antiquated system that subjugates women.

Yunus knew they could start at once, whether they were ready or not. He discovered that illiterate and uneducated women could

learn and wanted to learn and prosper in their own businesses. He
wanted to **empower people from the bottom up** and has done a
brilliant job. He teaches that everyone can create wealth and a lifetime of security. His mantra: *Start small, experiment, discover what
works, and then expand on it.*

Contrast that to American bankers who lent to purportedly
credit-worthy people with no real financial awareness, understanding or education about sound financial principles. We allowed
Wall Street greedaholics to create usurious wealth for themselves at
the expense of the many and the all.

The solution to our deep indebtedness, Yunus told us, is to take
one hundredth of the three trillion dollars in stimulus money, or
only 30 billion, and outreach the Grameen Bank principles. Then,
viola!—micro-businesses in America will bloom and boom and the
economy will be graciously revived, healthy, and moving again.
This can work worldwide and, in fact, inspired by Dr. Yunus.
micro-credit is actively working in over one hundred countries
now, including the U.S.A. Look for, and actively campaign for, a
Grameen Bank coming to your area. To see this at work, go to
www.grameenamerica.com.

It is thought that one man's trash is another man's cash.
Looks to us like American banks are closing at an extraordinary
rate. It is predicted that ultimately America will be like Canada,
with only seven banks left standing.

What if we quickly, safely, and satisfyingly take on the challenge
of thinking like MacGyver? We teach how the micro-credit system
works and its sound financial principles to failing bankers and to
people going bankrupt or going out of business. As instantly as possible, we institute micro-credit lending practices to individuals,
with five basic backers guaranteeing each and every loan. The key
question then arises: *"Can we raise ourselves by our bootstraps again
in this land of opportunity?"* We say the answer is a resounding *YES!*

At a recent lecture we attended in Hollywood, Dr. Yunus noted that we are both "selfish and selfless." So, we each need to create or find two kinds of businesses to participate in: one dedicated to making lots of profit for you, your family and your enterprise (*selfish*) and the other, a Social Enterprise dedicated to the service of others (*selfless*) and to solving a problem, without the initial intention of making money. With a selfish business you make money, and with a selfless business you save the world. Each of us has hidden inside us the deep desire to do both. Some of us did not know that we could SAVE THE WORLD STILL! Ask any kid and they will give you the shirt off their back (selfless). You still have that encoded in your DNA and we are here to remind you about it.

Doctor Yunus told us that thirty years ago, a woman borrowed money from Grameen Bank and created a successful micro-enterprise, then funded her daughter to become a medical doctor. Upon meeting with the mother and daughter, Yunus cried to himself, because the woman said, "Because of you, Dr. Yunus, I have a profitable business of my own, *and I became literate*—which I never thought was possible. Now I can read, and my daughter got a great education and beneficial skill set."

Yunus realized that the mother was equally bright, and under other circumstances could have become a doctor herself, with higher money-making potential. We need to ask the question: *"How many Einsteins are we missing because they are incarcerated in poverty due to the system?"* **Cynthia Kersey** (chapter ten) **is doing her part in building schools to educate the next Einstein.** (www.unstoppablefoundation.org) *What are you doing?*

"I was in France with Franck, the head of the great Dannon Yogurt Corporation," said Dr. Yunus. Franck asked Yunus what he could do to help Yunus with his passionate purposefulness. Yunus replied, "The children of Bangladesh are undernourished. I want you to create a yogurt that sells for essentially one penny and has all the vitamins, minerals, and nutrients a child needs. I want your manufacturing plant to be in Chittagong with Bengali employees, please."

Excitedly, Franck said: "Yes, I will do it, and make it in a biodegradable cup!"

"No!" exclaimed Yunus. "When I eat an ice cream cone, first, I eat the ice cream and then I eat the cone; there is no waste. My country already has a big solid waste problem."

This pushed the edge of Franck's imagination. He said, "We will work on it."

We predict that it will come to pass; that we will have clean, safe, *no-waste* food containers, thanks to Yunus's wisdom, questioning, probing and request, and to Franck's openness and willingness. Their creativity is motivating for many new social businesses. It will also serve Franck and the Dannon Corporation to stimulate breakthrough innovations that advance and greatly prosper his company —in ways both known and unknown.

The value of a man should be seen in what he gives and not in what he is able to receive. –Albert Einstein.

INSPIRED by Dr. Yunus's statement that he has working mini-solar machines that Bengali women use to charge cell phones, it triggered in Mark's mind the possibility of mini-desalination domes for Bengali women. Crystal Dwyer, Mark's beloved, is the creator of the health program *Living the Skinny Life* and the author of *Pure Thinking for Pure Results.* (www.crystaldwyer.com) Crystal heard Mark mention this concept, believed in it, and immediately added momentum to it. While driving home from Yunus's Hollywood appearance, they called John Pitre, one of the world's greatest inventors and artists and Mark's partner in Natural Power

Concepts (www.naturalpowerconcepts.com), and shared the idea with him.

Also inspired by this notion, John responded, "We can manufacture mini desalination condensation-collecting solar domes for an affordable cost."

The plan and desire is to offer these domes, with Grameen Bank doing the micro-credit financing, to millions of poor women everywhere. The units will give them pure, drinkable water every day and enough extra water to sell to their friends and neighbors at a profit.

Mark thought: If mini-solar cells could work for charging cell phone batteries profitably, why not have it work for mini-desalination domes? One Bengali woman could take ocean water, polluted water, or even stream water and use condensation to create pure, potable water. A three-foot diameter dome could easily generate 12+ glasses of water per day. Obviously, they can have several of these and have saleable water to their respective neighbors. The water would be pure, potable, localized, contaminate- and arsenic-free water for a very cheap price. (Arsenic water is a serious a problem for 35 million people in Bangladesh.)

This could begin to solve the water problems for the entire world.

Some people might think starting small and helping the poorest people of the world, people whom many consider insignificant, would have no impact on benefiting the world. However, this can be the proving ground for products that will reach into and touch every household on this planet. Clean available drinking water is one of the most significant challenges that await our solutions.

Anything that can successfully be done on a small scale can be expanded to a large scale and vice versa. More importantly, this type of enterprise stands on the underlying principle that what blesses one, blesses us all. John Locke, the philosophical inspirer of

President Thomas Jefferson, said: *"We need to do the most good, for the most people."*

CAN WE PAY OFF THE NATIONAL DEBT?

The easy answer is **yes**. We will show you how and make it palatable, though perhaps not tasty. The resistance is from the vested interests that are enshrined to absorb vast amounts of greedaholics' money.

Our friend Harry Dent, the renowned economist from Harvard, was the first to see the unprecedented boom back in the early 1990s in his book, *The Great Boom Ahead*. He looked at the rising spending of the massive Baby Boom generation and the information and technologies moving into the mainstream (such as autos, electricity and phones) from 1914 to 1929.

In his latest book, *The Great Depression Ahead*, Dent sees Baby Boomers shifting from spenders to savers and the deleveraging of the greatest credit and real estate bubble in modern history. He tells us that the government stimulus will ultimately fail and that financial systems will actually need to crash, like an alcoholic bottoming out before seeking help from Alcoholics Anonymous. This is the only way that the government will finally restructure our clearly unsustainable entitlement programs, and that voters will finally accept that. There is an old saying: "Never waste a good crisis."

The U.S. Treasury admits that the U.S. government has $46 trillion in unfunded liabilities for Medicare, Medicaid and Social Security. This is the reason the government is forecasting $trillion-plus deficits for years and decades to come—even in a good economy, which we won't see.

When Social Security started in 1935, only a small percentage of people lived past age 65, so it wasn't an economic burden. Now most people who reach retirement live into their 80s. We must start with a clean slate and begin with reforms such as moving the retirement age to 72, and raise it over time as life expectancy continues to rise. Working longer helps solve the demographic challenge of a slowing workforce and keeps people happier and healthier. 80% of that $46 trillion in unfunded liabilities come from health care, and more than 50% of those costs occur in the last 6 months of life. This obviously has to be dealt with, although that is a more complex issue.

We want you, dear reader, to create other solutions, in addition to and beyond these thought-starters.

Big ideas, no matter how crazy they may seem at first, have within them the seeds for a future harvest.

"People with wisdom are now at a point in which Chapter 11 for America is up for consideration. Collapse is not necessarily a bad thing. Starting over fresh in a new and good direction without baggage is good, and can have great advantages in the long run." We were told this by one of the all-time wise and great businessmen of our time, who prefers to remain anonymous.

There are many ways to do anything. We have read of scores of ways to quickly, safely and satisfyingly pay off the national debt. Ours is as follows:

Assume America is a person; we would sort of be like Donald Trump when he was walking down the street with his then-wife Marla Maples. He told her that the bum on the street was richer than he was. "Why?" Marla asked. Donald told her that he was four billion dollars upside down at the time, and Equitable and his other lenders were calling his loans. Trump reinvented himself in many ways, bankrupted a few of his companies, and then re-created him-

self, just like we have to do individually, collectively, and govern-
mentally. Today, Donald Trump is once again extremely successful
—a billionaire practitioner of unlimited possibilities.

Let's consider using the financial vehicle called Life Insurance,
one of the four most secure and venerated of financial tools. (This
is true because, until recently, the insurance business self-insured
itself and all its colleagues—so no insurance company ever went
bankrupt.) In this instance, life insurance is more accurately
referred to as death insurance.

1. Our idea is that every American buys a life insurance policy on
    him- or herself and their children living at home, with a face-
    value of thirty-five thousand dollars per person, to be paid out
    upon their death to the Federal Reserve, with a tax shelter ben-
    efit to be determined. The approximate cost of a policy on a
    thirty-year-old person would be about a dollar a day for a year,
    or $365. Obviously, people of different ages would be priced
    differently.

2. Another looming possibility is that the government uses some
    of our taxed income toward a life insurance policy on every
    living American, perhaps going heavier on individuals over fifty
    years of age because the payoff could be sooner. Equivalently,
    we use a dollar a day of taxation that is already being paid to
    buy insurance on every living American. That's approximately
    $305 million a day (305 million Americans) to buy a thirty-five
    thousand dollar death benefit policy paid to the Federal
    Reserve upon each individual's death.

Another iteration of this would be a $70,000 policy on each and
every individual with half going to their family or charity upon their
demise, and half to pay off the national debt. The point is, a sce-
nario can be devised that would make everyone happy, prosperous
and glad that the problem is being resolved.

When you divide 11 trillion dollars of American debt by our population of 305 million, it comes out that each of us owes about $35,000 to the national indebtedness. If each policy is scheduled to be irrevocably used for paying off the national debt via the Federal Reserve, over our human lifetimes, the debt vanishes and goes to zero, creating a strong dollar again.

Given our taxing system, we can afford to give each person who invests in a policy (or if they are wealthy, several such policies) a tax break of two dollars for every dollar permanentized in life insurance payable only to the Federal Reserve.

This would create a fully solvent economy that starts back at zero. We are willing to be spokespeople for this colossal idea and feel confident that the life insurance industry would love to pay us to do it.

The Federal Reserve would need to agree to the idea of using these policies to reinvent our financial system, and would need to stop charging usurious interest once this plan is agreed to, in place, and working. Within less than one hundred years, our country would be totally debt free. We can see that once we embrace this grand and noble idea and put it in motion, everyone would exhale a sigh of relief and go back to being on purpose about their lives and business pursuits.

Of course, politicians have to become accountable and stop spending our tomorrows without our consent in writing.

Big ideas get the engine of ingenuity revved up.

Consider This: The Stimulus Package

Another BIG idea—*what if* the American government created an additional stimulus package? The government has a three-trillion-dollar initial stimulus package, the effect of which is pretty much invisible to most of us. The hoped-for effect was that it would slow the recession and re-ignite the economy. As of this writing, it has not yet achieved its hoped-for result.

So, *what if* the government took an additional three trillion dollars, because the Federal Reserve can print up as much as it wants, and gave $10,000 to each living American, with the proviso that it be spent in America for American goods and services? Part of this amount would be used to fund the life insurance idea that was previously proposed. *Could this be a stimulus that causes instantaneous behavioral change in individuals and business, and re-launches a healthy and fear-free economy?*

Does this spark ideas from you? Ask yourself the great starter question of *What if* … and let your imagination take you on a journey of solutions. Write them down and share them with your like minded friends who want to make a difference. Who knows, maybe *you* have the best answer, and it will be broadcast and implemented to everyone's benefit.

This simple embraceable idea could catch on like wildfire, making America debt-free, stress-free and set-free economically, to again be a visionary leader that actually leads.

There are four big economic engines that historically are the foundation of America's giant wealth. They include, but are not limited to: the auto industry, real estate, banks, and the life insurance industry about which we have spoken above.

THE AUTOMOTIVE INDUSTRY

In the adventure with AO, you learned that 1906 was the year America broke free of the first Great Depression of 1898. We

clearly got the American economy going with three major innovations: the automobile, petroleum, and airplane flight. Given that
petroleum became available to replace whale oil, thanks to the
refining efforts of Henry Morrison Flagler and his partner and co-
founder John D. Rockefeller, of what became Standard Oil, we
could have gas-driven automobiles invented in America by Henry
Ford. Ford's automobile mass production blossomed into the economic wonder that sold over 14,000,000 cars in one year. We now
know that the automobile industry employs one in ten Americans,
which includes manufacturing, distribution, sales, gas stations,
repair shops, road construction, et al.

Our thinking is that if it happened before, it can happen again.
Let's look at the innovation of electric cars that work as well as gas-
driven cars. For example, cars from www.BetterPlace.com are offer
exciting new possibilities. Their vision was to create a virtual oil
field with an integrated renewable energy smart-grid technology
and switchable batteries that would be for the mass market, go
ever-greater distances, and are as fast as gas guzzlers.

Let's assume the great successes that Better Place has had in
Israel and Denmark can also happen here in America. We can experience the reinvention of the automobile industry and re-invigorate
the entire economy.

If we sold fourteen million new cars at $30,000 each, that's $720
billion. Add in electric charging stations at approximately $1.5 mil-
lion each and **you quickly reinvigorate the economy with a trillion dollars in real cash flow.** This was done in one year by Henry
Ford and can be done again, if we put the political stamp of
approval on it, and ask the unions to rethink how they can allow
this new business to have room to breathe and come to life for the
long-term benefit of all of us. This will start a velocity wave of
money. We believe this can happen with a new breed of electric
cars made by a variety of companies.

Innovations are always considered disruptive technologies in the beginning. They are ultimately embraced and soon universally accepted after a trial basis.

Historically, the slogan has been: *"As goes General Motors, so goes America."* General Motors is clearly broken, from an antiquated business model and stodgy thinking. It is absorbing vast amounts of government cash to run yesterday's thinking, models, technology and ideas. We think new ideas, innovations, and car creations are demanded by a hungry marketplace that no longer wants fuel-burning, petrochemical-eating cars when we can have cars that are easy on the environmental, less expensive, longer lasting and cost effective.

These electric cars can also be charged—think re-fueled—by alternative energy generating stations powered by wind, thermal, solar, geothermal, and tidal forces, all of which require new infrastructure construction, creating millions of jobs. Jobs are the real energizer of the economy; more high paying, substantial jobs equal a real, strong and vital economy.

REAL ESTATE

Real estate is clearly the biggest money business in America. Google says one could buy all the residential real estate in America for $23.5 trillion dollars. This is half of the highest retail price before the crash, for two reasons: One, Americans used their homes as piggy banks or an ATM machine, and two, many unqualified and financially unstable people were allowed to buy homes.

We need to educate and qualify new home buyers with training programs that are as thoroughly and competently delivered as driver's education classes. Given the breakthroughs in technology with generation 4 phones, it is possible to train many people on the phone, have them finally carded to insure it 's really them, then tested at a special certified center to give them their homebuyer certificate of approval. We need a company that does homeownership counseling and qualification. Most would-be buyers don't know where to begin. We need an independent company with no association to banks. This company can qualify and certify would-be homeowners.

The company will effectively teach the individuals buying a home or real estate what they can really afford and how much of a loan they can seek. This would better qualify the buyer to banks. Individuals would be more educated and would make better buying decisions. It would create a truer market. This could become a really large business or franchise. The products would have more integrity and be financially sound. The key is that companies have to be independent of banks and have no conflicts of interest in their certification process. This idea alone could get the economy going.

Harry Dent suggested to us that the government orchestrate a $20 trillion write-down in private debt. In addition to the $46 trillion in unfunded liabilities for entitlements, we have $42 trillion in private debt that mushroomed $23 trillion from 2000-2008. That is 3.2 times the $13 trillion (and rising) in federal debt. This private debt rose largely around the unprecedented bubble in real estate prices. The government could give assistance only to banks that write down loans for consumers and businesses. We need to eliminate this excessive $20 trillion-plus in debt by forcing banks to write loans down to market value.

How do we accomplish that without a massive run on the banks like in the early 1930s? The government agrees to take on something like 30% of the debt write-offs (the minimum possible to let the best banks survive) and the banks take 70%. Dent calls this "The Ultimate Stimulus Program," as $20 trillion less in debt would save consumers and businesses more than $1 trillion a year, for decades into the future! And the debt the government takes over would have lower interest rates. Dent reminds us that the banks and Wall Street simply went nuts in creating the greatest bubble in debt and real estate in modern history. Only a crisis and fresh ideas will allow us to return government and private debt back to reality, so that the next generation can have affordable housing, interest rates and debt levels again. That is the only basis for a strong and sustainable recovery in an era where demographic trends for the U.S. and all developed countries are not as strong as they used to be.

The last choice for the housing problem is to do what they do in China. The employer provides housing only to those who work and keep working. This obviously has inherent dangers. We like free enterprise because we are free to succeed or fail. It is up to the individual. The good news with free enterprise is that you can try and re-try until you succeed, earn enough money for a proper down payment, and then buy a home, which is still the beloved American dream.

BANKS

Assuming Harry Dent's idea of a government paying twenty trillion stimulus package to the BEST banks has happened. We must know that banks are currently holding 5,000,000 off the books in bank-held, hidden foreclosures, because they don't want to be bankrupted with bad paper. If Dent's idea happened, most of those foreclosures would be absorbed. This could be a boost of $1.5 trillion to the economy as it is fully experienced.

When banks are repaid on their loans of $1.5 trillion, they are able to, and have the legal ability to lend on a ten-to-one ratio, which would make $15 trillion instantly available for business loans, residential and commercial real estate. The economic system can start to work again.

Debit Cards

To insure their solvency, banks have taken back credit cards and further limited individuals lines of credit—without telling them. This has been done to reduce credit card companies' exposure to bad loans. Additionally, more than 1.6 million people per year, as we write this, are going bankrupt, an all time high that further exacerbates the financial crisis. The reasons are many and varied: a bad economy, lavish living, medical expenses, divorce, etc.

Mark, in an attempt to help and serve the unbanked, starting with his faithful housekeeper, got the first personally sponsored MasterCard debit card. Today everyone needs a debit card, and his company can issue one almost immediately to individuals who give a $150 deposit. Once they have a card, they can load it at any bank, credit union, and at most ATM machines around the world.

Through his enterprise, Mark plans to teach financial literacy with every debit card. His outrageous dream is that when individuals receive a debit card, they also receive financial literacy training in order to become financially solvent and economically viable.

Eighty-two percent of the world's population is unbanked, uneducated, and do not have credit; and as Dr. Yunus says, "Credit is a fundamental human right." Debit cards that can morph into credit cards, over time and with proper handling, expand the possibilities of all that life has to offer.

As this process gains momentum, people who have previously hidden their finances, say in a mattress or a *Prince Albert* can or wherever, can suddenly begin building credit. They can come to understand the system of banks; banking can again be trusted, and the velocity of money starts anew. We saw that the banker to the poor, Dr. Yunus, got people to believe in financial possibilities, and that women could be great and inspiring business entrepreneurs.

We can see this reach out progressively to serve 5.6 billion unbanked people, and the cash they are stashing or hiding in a black market will come into the system and start to circulate again.

We began this book talking about Jules Verne's "crazy ideas" more than 150 years ago, when he wrote that "people would fly above the ground, rocket into space, dive and stay under the water and be able to breathe and not drown, and burrow into the earth." It has all happened and much, much more.

We see the triangle as:

1. *fiction* (imagination) starts the process, moving to
2. *theory*, which makes it believable—the Wright Brothers proving that lift and drag gives heavier-than-air vehicles the ability to fly, and finally
3. *fact*, aviation became a reality and manifested itself because Jules Verne wrote and inspired belief in the Wright Brothers, who launched aviation.

Likewise, Mark wants to create a Debit-to-Credit Revolution: the poor receive debit cards and financial literacy training, and become able to master money and finance, rather than have it master them and their lives and lifestyles. ***Ask yourself: What happens when five-plus billion people have debit, and ultimately credit, available?*** They have their potential and reality vastly expanded, to be expressed as the full use of their talents and abilities.

Credit determines whether you have the financial ability to do things, simple things like purchasing food on an airplane. Just the issuance of a MasterCard debit card with $150 on it, as in the case of the micro-credit business, can potentially generate more than a trillion dollars a year in new business, if usage is expanded worldwide.

The advantage of a debit card is that the owner cannot spend more than they have first put on it or what is called 'loaded', which determines the card's value.

An additional big advantage is that money transfers can be made internationally and instantly from America to loved ones' "companion cards" in their home countries. For example, many Hispanics send home an average of $250 monthly. The costs and problems of transferring this money are usurious and time consuming, and it can get stolen or delayed. The benefit of companion cards is that they will cheerfully create as many as requested, up to twelve. In this example, the Hispanic-American puts two hundred and fifty dollars on the card here and that amount is immediately available on the companion card so that their loved one has it instantly, and for a dollar and fifty cents rather than the forty dollars charged by the exploitive systems currently available.

Are you ready to express your idea to benefit others?

ALTERNATIVE INCOME ENERGY

Alternative Income Energy is the solution to getting the world to work. Mark's great and inspiring intellectual mentor and teacher was Dr. R. Buckminster Fuller. "Bucky" Fuller was arguably Einstein's best student and an American engineer, architect, designer, inventor, author and futurist, probably best known for his geodesic domes. Fifty years ago, Fuller said that America and the world need fifty-year plans to really succeed and to make humanity economically and physically successful.

Mark had a chance to speak with businessman and politician Mitt Romney at a dinner, and asked about Chinese ownership of American equities and real estate. To Mark's surprise, Mitt answered, "The Chinese have a fifty-year plan to enforce ***authoritarian capitalism***. We have no plan!"

We, your beloved authors, want the ideas outlined in this book to start you thinking about fifty years of crystal-clear plans for yourself, your company, your family, and our government.

As a futurist, Bucky looked fifty years into the future with his concept called: **World Game**™ or how to make the world economically and physically successful for one hundred percent of humanity. Fuller wrote a book about this called **Utopia or Oblivion**. Fifty years ago he suggested that ecology and the economy would be in trouble, as they are, and gave wise insights into what to do about it.

Five decades ago he correctly predicted that we would need to switch our economy from having nothing back a dollar (except the faith and integrity of America) because we went off the Gold Standard during the Nixon presidency. Fuller conceived and recommended that we go on the EU standard, meaning Energy Units Standard. Energy units could become the standard of exchange for money for the entire world. America has the inventions, ideas, people, and the most natural resources in the world to quickly create **income energy—solar, wind, tidal, and geothermal**—as the basis of our ever-expanding economy.

Fuller envisioned a world run on income energy from solar, wind, tidal and geothermal sources. Each of these inventions are heavily patented in America, with the most patents held by Natural Power Concepts.

Fuller dreamed of, designed and wanted a world-around electrical energy grid, with energy shared from time zone to time zone, so it would not be revved up on the East Coast and an hour later revved up in the Midwest and ground-volted on the East Coast, and so on, around the world. This concept can be seen online at www.geni.org, the Global Electric Network Institute site (GENI). Located there are pictures of Fuller's imaginative Dymaxion Map, with overlays of what a fully functioning electrical grid would look like. Fuller envisioned energy abundance via available technology, and stated these benefits to realizing his concept:

* increase everyone's standard of living
* reduce fossil fuel demand and the resultant pollution
* relieve the population explosion
* reduce world hunger
* reduce deforestation, topsoil loss, and spreading of deserts
* enhance world trade
* promote international cooperation and peace

The benefits of Fuller's electrical grid are enormous and the investment is relatively small. What is lacking is the leadership of a John F, Kennedy, who said, *"Let's land a man on the moon."* Ideas and ideals like this are positive, exciting, momentous, humanity uplifting, courageous, and job-creating on a vast scale. Fuller's idea is of equal or greater magnitude and benefit as landing a man on the moon, and it serves everyone. Our dream is that many readers agree and encourage politicians around the world to work together and make it happen.

Now is the appointed time and we can do this if we have the will to do it!

ALTERNATIVE ENERGY

We can now discuss the Alternative Energy creation by the individual, the company and the government. The time for **Alternative Income Energy** has come. We need to get off the self-starter system of our world's petrochemicals.

Solar energy exists, both photovoltaic and thermal. Photovoltaic is the direct conversion of light into electricity at the atomic level, called solar cells, and is being used now on residential homes as well as by industry, in areas of high incidence of solar energy.

Solargenix is the largest solar thermal power plant ever to be built, located in Boulder City, Nevada, at a cost of about five billion dollars. (www.solargenix.com)

Wind energy from windmills has been around for centuries and is only now coming into its own. One company with the Leonardo da Vinci of our time, John Pitre, the world's number one living surrealist artist, (www.johnpitre.com) has created and patented ten wind-driven inventions. Pitre's company, Natural Power Concepts (NPC), is a Hawaii-based think tank with more than a 101 original and innovative inventions.

For the OshKosh company, Pitre has created a mobile windmill that can energize 1,000 homes in a small military encampment or rural area with prevailing winds of 12 miles an hour or more. For cities, he has invented four roof top machines that effectively capture wind at the top or sides of buildings at a rate of 52% effectiveness, where no other device has been more than 8% effective.

The question: Can we get the water we need without robbing our petrochemical capital accounts wastefully?

Pitre and his team's biggest breakthrough, one that will change the world, uses **tidal energy to purify water**. Tidal energy is nonintermittent and pulsates between nine and twelve feet every nine seconds. In John's invention, ocean water pulsates through a turbine, essentially creating free energy. The energy is used to push the water through a reverse osmotic membrane that Pitre innovated, and viola! Pure, clean, drinkable desalinated water. This is necessary because the amount of drinkable water on the planet is now at .007%. Naysayers predict that the next wars will be over water, which now costs more per gallon than gasoline.

In Saudi Arabia, water is desalinated with energy from gasoline; the cost is one gallon of gasoline to make one gallon of water. Gasoline is cheap and relatively abundantly in Saudi Arabia, though it still pollutes and damages the environment. In a closed system like Saudi Arabia's, where oil is cheap, abundant and easily available, that may be okay. We have discovered that oil is limited in total supply, expensive and toxic to our entire environment.

When considering the total cost accounting of oil, we must consider that it took a hundred and sixty million years for Mother Nature to create that one gallon of oil. We burn it like that doesn't matter and it is nothing, like we can instantly replace it. We also must account for pouring burnt hydrocarbons into the atmosphere and stratosphere that are creating the greenhouse effect, and thus global warming. As a result, the water level at our shores is rising and flooding many costal communities, as evidenced in Hawaii, Manhattan, Mumbai, the Maldives and around the world.

Pitre's desalination buoys have one simple anchor and float two miles offshore. They are aesthetically pleasing and instantly functional, using reverse osmosis membranes to purify the water. The water can then be piped where it is needed or put in a giant bladder in a container ship and transported. After the cost of the structure itself and a modest maintenance charge, it produces inexpensive water virtually forever.

A 134-foot diameter desalination plant at sea can produce 200 million gallons of fresh, pure, clean, drinkable water a year. Several of these linked together could supply all the needs of a major city such as Los Angeles, Mumbai, or Mexico City. The Bible promises that we shall make deserts bloom; now we have the technological invention to do just that ... and to supply abundant jobs, food, and an ever more exciting future.

The world's population in the last century has gone from about a billion people to seven billion. If our leadership in government and business think this through, what is really needed is water. Realizing this, **America could create energy and water for everyone,** and thus **create unlimited jobs** with a new infrastructure, rather than trying to mend what clearly is not working and will not work again.

Let's go to Trinidad, a small Caribbean island with oil wealth, but a depleted water aquifer. An aquifer is the water supply for wells and springs, and thus the source of the drinking water of the population. When Mark spoke with representatives of the University of the West Indies, he and his family were invited to meet with the incoming Prime Minister and dine with his cabinet. Mark viewed a PowerPoint presentation about water as a worldwide problem, and especially problematic for small islands surrounded by ocean water. It brings to mind the poem we all read in high school English literature: "**Water, water everywhere and not a drop to drink**," by Samuel Coleridge in "The Rime of the Ancient Mariner."

The bottom and top line is that water can be made abundantly and inexpensively available to source and serve Trinidad and everywhere, now. Water is only a finite commodity because we have not fundamentally decided to make it an infinite commodity. Water, in our opinion, is a basic human right, and a change in thinking will cause a change in results.

In Mumbai, the aquifers are dehydrated and sucking in salt water from the sea. In Mexico, the water table has dropped fifteen feet in the last decade. These are but a few of many examples that you will see pop up more and more. It is time to make a difference, to stand up for more than enough water now.

THE GAME CHANGER: SOLAZYME

The biggest problems in the world today are energy, hunger & food, and clean water. Solazyme's revolutionary new processes can be a big part of the new solution.

Micro-algae is the new oil. Just as petrochemicals took the place of whale oil, we predict that petrochemicals will be replaced with micro-algae produced oil. We know that we are running out of easy-to-obtain oil and that is now very expensive to harvest.

Use of this new oil is **inevitable, transformational**, and **in alignment with the resources available**—meaning that the six-trillion-dollar oil infrastructure can instantly be converted to carrying oil made of algae. There is no mixing or matching; it is the total, safe, and **green replacement** for oil. The bonus is that it helps to reduce the carbon footprint made by 150 years of hydrocarbon usage, in every good way.

Solazyme (www.solazyme.com)has pioneered, innovated, explored and discovered what 200 other companies, including Exxon's $300-million-dollar investment, could not: micro-algae that grows high quality, clean, and ready-to-use oil. The San Francisco-based company has developed methods to create different types of oil by using a variety of 14,000 algae strains, which offer more applications than ethanol and use lower amounts of effort, water, and land mass.

In January of 2008, Solazyme partnered with Chevron Technology Ventures to commercialize the algae fuel and to work with the US Department of Energy's National Renewable Energy Laboratory. They are also carrying out fuel analysis to certify its worthiness for aviation use. Additionally, they create heart-healthy, vegetarian, protein-rich micro-algae cookies, supplements and vitamins, now sold at stores such as Whole Foods. They work with Unilever to create and distribute renewable, sustainable personal care products like soap and cosmetics. Algae is a multi-talented, amazing performer with almost unlimited promise.

Jonathan Wolfson, CEO, says he can produce large volumes of oil, now. Micro-algae self-replicates virtually overnight. In a YouTube video, Wolfson states that starting with only two algae, they can grow to more than 100,000 liters of oil in three days. In a test conducted onboard a U.S. Navy ship, they produced 20,000 gallons of fuel in the first half of the year, as part of an $8.5 million dollar contract.

Even in the worst credit crunch ever, venture capitalists are giving gigantic amounts of money to Solazyme because they make good economic sense. They can see the need and the fact that Solazyme has the leading solution, *now*.

THE X PRIZE FOUNDATION

Recently we were invited to a phenomenal group meeting run by Keith Ferrazzi, author of ***Never Eat Alone*** and founder of Big Task Weekends, a meeting of the Who's Who of movers, shakers and moneymakers from around the country and the world. Early in the evening, as we were meeting and greeting people, we were introduced to the founder and chairman of the famed X PRIZE, Dr. Peter Diamandis. Peter is dedicated; his X PRIZE Foundation has the wisest group of enlightened trustees that we have seen anywhere. Their cause: "Revolution Through Competition."

From their website: "The X PRIZE Foundation Board of Trustees consists of visionaries and luminaries who recognize the power of prize philanthropy to create fundamental change in the world. The mission of the X PRIZE Foundation is to bring about radical breakthroughs for the benefit of humanity. We do this by creating and managing prizes that drive innovators to solve some of the greatest challenges facing the world today.

"The X PRIZE is viewed as the leading model to leverage the elements of public interest, entrepreneurial spirit and cross-disciplinary innovation to bring about breakthroughs that benefit us all.

"We believe that a small group of people with passion for a cause can achieve that which has never been attained. This is why we stage competitions that challenge issues that matter most. An X PRIZE is a $10 million+ award given to the first team to achieve a specific goal, set by the X PRIZE Foundation, which has the potential to benefit humanity. Rather than awarding money to honor past achievements or directly funding research, an X PRIZE incites innovation by tapping into our competitive and entrepreneurial spirits."

To date, they charge an entry fee to participate in attempting to win the X PRIZE, so the project is basically self-funding-to-profitable. This concept and its underlying principle can be used to stimulate solutions in the form of challenges at any level—your family, business, charity, local neighborhood, community, our country or the world. We believe that more like-minded, inspired masterminds working in the spirit of cooperative harmony, challenged with a definite major objective, can solve both your problems and the world's problems.

You can be one of these people. It can even start with you. You could either start your own deal, join the X PRIZE team membership at their website (www.xprize.org), or be open and available to something around you.

THE FIRST SUPPER

Consider this: Warren Buffet, the world's richest investor and Bill Gates, the world's richest man with the world's richest foundation, decided to bring together the forty richest people in the world to inspire them to give away half of their multi-billions of accumulated wealth to do philanthropic good for the entire world and all of humanity.

Fortune Magazine, July 12, 2010, an article entitled ***The $600 Billion Dollar Challenge*** describes the kick-off of a campaign dedicated to inspiring billionaires to gift half their accumulated wealth and riches to charity. Buffet and Gates are asking billionaires to pledge to give away at least half of their wealth during their lifetimes or at death. As the campaign succeeds, it will change philanthropy and the world. More meetings are planned, after their "First Supper."

Guess who came to dinner? Oprah Winfrey, Eli and Edythe Broad, Ted Turner, David Rockefeller, Chuck Feeney, Mayor Michael Bloomberg, George Soros, Julian Robertson, John and Tashia Morgridge and Pete Peterson, to name a few.

This meeting of the richest of the rich was dubbed the "biggest fundraising drive in history" and dedicated to changing philanthropic behavior of the wealthiest of the wealthy and be an inspiration to others to give greatly. The goal is to get the super-rich on the *Forbes* list of the 400 wealthiest Americans to pledge and give at least fifty percent of their net worth during their lifetimes or at death. The list of attendees' value is now $1.2 trillion, so the colossal goal of half is $600 billion, and that is only their beginning desire.

Buffet has personally pledged to give away all of his Berkshire Hathaway stock to the philanthropic foundation. He says, "I couldn't be happier with that decision." Of gifts to his own children, Buffet has always said, *"I want to give them enough to do something, but not enough to do nothing."*

To get a real feel for these two giants, watch the video of Charlie Rose interviewing Warren Buffet across the course of one entire year. We suspect that you will be wowed, inspired and thankful to have listened to and watched the man Charlie says is the "brightest businessman with the most integrity ever." Additionally, watch the Gates-Buffet day at Washington University. These are available online, at Netflix or Blockbuster.

Process number one: Here's what we want you to consider. **Pretend you are either Gates or Buffet.***Who would you invite?* Assume everyone, worldwide, is available and will come because you call. *What would you say? Write out your exact speech.* Warren and Bill both had their personal philanthropic pledges in writing and ready to hand out, as validation that giving does not hurt—rather, it expands, improves, and enhances your soul and life in every good way. *What would you recommend they all do?* Really think through your request. You have within you gigantic desires that this very process can set on fire. *Can you think big enough and challenge yourself to be your highest and best self?*

Now, let's bring the model into your reality. Why not invite your seven to ten most enlightened friends to your home or apartment. Shut off the television and **tell-your-vision** to your assembled Dream Team. Ask them how much they could give or inspire, as Gates and Buffet did, to get others to give. Dream big! Imagination is free and available increasingly as you use it.

Process number two: Perhaps you don't want anyone to visit your home, office, or favorite eatery with you. Then set aside some time, play some relaxing Steven Halpern music, go inside the theater of your mind and imagine giving away a billion dollars of your own, with the obvious goal to do the most good and the least harm with it. You want to make a difference that makes a difference and that leaves a lasting, impactful, permanent and sustainable, legacy-generating difference. You can change the world, if you have the desire, thinking, and self-initiative-to-action plan. You can put together an irresistibly powerful dream team of like-minded, let's-make-it-happen partners.

Process number three: We are encouraging and exciting you to think like you've never thought before. Awaken your full potential, resources, talents, and abilities. If you knew you could make the world work for one hundred percent of humanity, helping make them economically and physically successful, *what would you do?* Nothing is stopping you. We give you permission to exercise your comprehensive source-generated sense of being.

Process number four: *What if* we could create a master plan for the **Biggest Thinkers Supper**, a gathering of 10,000. Like the Woodstock Music Festival, which brought out the greatest musicians of the time, we would bring the wisest thinkers of our time, all dedicated to solving the biggest financial crisis of all time. For Woodstock, when people raised their vibration they attracted others on that level and brought about an enlightened musical gathering. Now we can have an enlightened let's-make-the-world-successful gathering.

The richest/brightest/most committed/dedicated/make-it-happen-people from around the world would love to come together for a purpose greater than them. Until now this wasn't possible; before now we didn't know who they were, had no place to hold them or transportation to bring them together, nor the technology to connect them all and keep them connected. Now we have webinars, Skype, a wide assortment of technological tools, and the awareness of superstars in each country who could be enrolled in a super-supper event.

You can create the second supper. No one person or group can solve all the problems of the world. However, a high-quality mastermind group can conceptually put forth a brilliant plan that if acted upon, can generate positive results far into the future.

Now, what can you predict? We predict that you will expand your life, thinking, joy, and future happiness. Perhaps then you, too, can become the next Dr. Yunus and you, too, can win the Noble Peace Prize, with original thinking and life-changing work.

What if all of the ideas we wrote about to get the economy rocking … literally stimulate hundreds, if not thousands, of ideas? *What if* even more ideas were generated and taken into serious, action-oriented think tanks that wisely accept, process and decide on action steps to sequentially and successfully implement the ideas?

You know what? The world could work for everyone, everywhere.

Fairfield, Iowa

Hidden in the heartland of America is Camelot. Camelot, as you remember, is the idyllic city where everyone is healthy, happy, prosperous, on-purpose, in love, with a perfect and wise government, and life is romantically magical and mystical. T.H. White wrote *The Once and Future King* about the legend of King Arthur, which became a great, must-see Broadway musical and movie called *Camelot*.

Iowa has a "City of Light" called Fairfield, a little city with a population of 9,509 people. Many practice a meditation technique and technology called TM, Transcendental Meditation. TM is an art, science, and practice founded by Maharishi Mahesh Yogi, frequently called the Beatle's Guru. Using a special practice of meditation, Maharishi promises that it is everyone's birthright to have unlimited energy, intelligence, and happiness. The high promise of TM is to create a peaceful, harmonious world now and for all future generations to enjoy. Mark felt that visiting Fairfield was like visiting Camelot.

The Maharishi's University and center of the TM Universe is in Fairfield. The TM population has blossomed with thoughtful, creative, entrepreneurial people using TM as an active practice, life and lifestyle. It out-pictures as a peaceful, stress free, and conscious place to live, love, grow, prosper and develop. The people there are striving for enlightenment, joy and success; they help each other be all that they can be. They express and experience kindness to one another and to all the visitors, which are many.

Fairfield has been called the Silicon Valley and the Entrepreneurial Capital of Iowa. It boasts more Inc. 500 companies than any city of its size, and more restaurants per capita than San Francisco. As a hotbed of entrepreneurship, the city leaders cheerfully mentor and help all who want to prosper and grow their wealth. Leadership of Fairfield is visionary and exciting as a small rural community that works, thanks to Mayor Ed Malloy. Ed is a rare, thoughtful, positive politician, a make-it-happen kind of guy. Mayor Malloy is also an owner of a successful, active oil brokerage business.

Ed works closely with Dr. John Hagelin, an astrophysicist trained at Harvard. Hagelin loves and actively practices TM. He is an outstanding teacher, leader, and inspiration for the students, faculty and visiting luminaries at the university. Dr. Hagelin travels relentlessly, speaking eloquently and articulately about consciousness, the cosmos, and their practical relevance to daily life. His passionate presentations encourage the entire TM community and all others to become consciously enlightened, reaping the rewards of greater health and wisdom.

TM creates a state of mental coherence that is demonstrable and helps to make practicing individuals calm, creative, loving, resourceful, and better able to use their full talents, skills, and abilities. While in Fairfield, Mark toured the elementary, junior high, high school, and university. He witnessed that ten minutes of TM practiced twice per day has produced the most blissful, happy, and wise students he has ever seen, anywhere. This, from a man who travels around the world 250,000 miles per year, speaking and entrepreneuring!

The Mayor's home is where all the visiting dignitaries and who's who of the world stay when they are in the neighborhood. Mayor Ed hosted Mark and one of his writing partners, Jack Canfield, co-authors of the *Chicken Soup for Soul* series, while they were in Fairfield to receive an award. The Mayor has a lovely home designed in spectacular Vedic Architecture. Mark immediately befriended Ed for his glorious conversational wisdom and eclectic insightfulness. He thought the world of Ed's brilliance and thoughtful hospitality.

It's recommended that everyone put a visit to Fairfield, Iowa on their respective *bucket list*. When there, tour the university campus, the idyllic downtown, and stop by the Mayor's office and say hello. You will experience a community working in harmony. The welcome you receive in this rural intellectual community will give you faith and hope that contrary to media reports, the American Dream is alive, well, and thriving.

> *If you think you are HERE in the problem and trying to get OVER THERE to the solution, that's a long way to go. When you are aware that you are not separated from your Creative Source, you have arrived at the doorstep of the solution.*

THE MONEY MANIFESTATION MINDSET

Many people harbor the belief that those who succeed in business are cold and uncaring and live only for the pursuit of profit. We would like to share with you the mindset and heartset of an extraordinary businessman who has achieved great success and humbly wishes to remain anonymous. These are his words:

"Making money is in your head, not anywhere else. Expectation and joy equal manifestation energy. We are here to continue a good work, the work of creation. I expect God to bless my efforts to make money, but only because it is good. It is for the completion of the good work. What you do with money is for the completion of creation, and for that I expect the universe to cooperate with me to deliver the money with which God has blessed me this day to make for the purpose of completing His creation."

This concept for him was a paradigm shift from believing that making money or the pursuit of making money was a sin—and when he made this shift in thought, money became instantaneously more plentiful in his experience.

He continues, "Our natural condition is our experiencing the universe working together for our good. Success is our natural condition. If you don't have it, it's because you are hindering it, like the sandbags on a hot air balloon. You must loose these sandbags of fear, greed, ambition, anxiety and rise up into the air currents of your natural flow. Don't walk upstream and fight the current; blend with the water and float downstream with the flow. Ancient tribal wisdom says that an Indian is like a drop of rain that falls in the stream and naturally goes with the flow and is at peace, while a white man struggles upstream and makes less distance with more stress. You only lose money when you don't go with the flow.

"Money has nothing to do with education or a business plan—it's a state of mind. It's a spiritual experience. I was put here to succeed, that's my natural state. God put me in this state. My job is to recognize that. Most people don't have success because they don't believe it is their place and purpose. You must recognize your place and purpose and claim them. God expects me to be successful. You can't learn it or teach it, it just is.

"In the Garden of Eden, they were going with the flow until they took other suggestions. Jesus said he would restore us to that state. To be born again is to be reinstated. A man's natural state is in harmony with the universe, and if you are living in that state, you are in the Garden of Eden. This is atonement—at one with the universe.

"The universe conspires to bless me every day. The universe conspires to make you prosperous if you have the right purpose in mind. Fully expect that this day will bring you a blessing. I fully expect that and anticipate with joy its arrival."

His success in business is constant, and what is so encouraging is that it is so natural, like the unfolding of a flower, almost effortless. He is happily convinced it is the mindset that he embraces that bears such profitable fruit—and we are too. We share his thoughts with you so you can naturally receive abundantly by getting into the flow of God's plan for you.

When the solution is simple, God is answering. –Albert Einstein

Solutions await your vital creations.

You, our beloved reader, are now encouraged to bloom where you are planted. The problems are not bigger than we are, because we are all in the solution together. It is the validation that fables can be real and that living Joyously-In-Spirit and being Source-Inspired, is a Soulution that works.

So … **Go forth and be the Soulution, for U R the Solution!**

13

AFTERWORD

U R your imagination, out-pictured. Your life and life-style are the result of your thinking. You can change your thinking and change your life, lifestyle and future. This is what AO has been teaching the kids, this and the law of attraction, throughout our fable.

A fable, of course, is something that never was and always will be, like a myth. It is a story you enjoy and are compelled to read, re-read, and then be inspired to tell all your friends to read, which we hope you do.

We want the world to work. We decided that if we could inspire you to think anew, that *you* would be the one to perhaps change your world, and thereby change our world for the better. It was a deliciously and deliriously big assignment we gave ourselves, and if you have read this far, you implicitly agree with our premise. Our world wants to work. It is set up to be "friendly," as Einstein said, and together, using the principle that we shared in the story, we can make it so!

We thank you for reading our first ***AO Adventure*** and hope you are desirous of reading more. As Mark did with the *Chicken Soup for the Soul* series and Bill did with *MacGyver* and nine other TV series, we hope you will enjoy our proposed future sequels and pre-quels. Hopefully you will also want to watch, as we bring it to the big screen with our friend Darby Angel, of AngelWorld Entertainment.

We write because we love to tell great and inspiring stories and we love you for participating in ours.

Thank you, our beloved reader!

Mark and Bill

14

THE AFTERWORD AFTER THE AFTERWORD

An Invitation

No writer has ever, to our knowledge, written a Preface to the Preface, like we did, and now to conclude our blatant originality, we finish with an Afterword after the Afterword.

The Big Ideas!

We have told you that **your imagination creates your reality.** It does that when you are in the *joy-in-spirit.* Being in the joy of spirit allows you to communicate and commune with the infinite. It is easiest to go into what is called "the secret place of the most high" when you are in a quiet place with peaceful music playing, meditatively listening to your joy-of-spirit. Allow it to direct, inform, and lead you. You can personally be in direct communication with infinite intelligence and you do not need an intermediary. That said, if you get an opportunity to attend one of our many seminars in which we lead a meditation, you will be enchanted to raise your vibration and achieve attainment of your joy-of-spirit.

As you discipline yourself to live, move and keep your being in the joy-in-spirit, your awareness will automatically grow, develop, and expand. You will go into life and see, as Einstein said: "*We live in a friendly universe.*"

The Universe conspires to source and serve you when you are in a joy-filled state-of-being. Universe can work best for you when you are in this joy-filled state, and seemingly works against you when you are not. As you send out joy, you are fulfilled thrice: You feel good as you send out joy, you feel good when you catch up to the good feelings and vibrations that you emanated outward, and you remember your seconds, minutes, hours, days, weeks, months, years, and entire lifetime as one of utter and absolute joy. Joy is your natural, high spiritual state.

Joy inspires awareness. Expanded awareness invites you to see possibilities that you could not previously see. Awareness ignites desire. Desire is the beginning of all creation and allows you to rise metaphorically higher and higher. Desire prompts bold steps of action. White-hot, continually cultivated desire ultimately out-pictures as results.

When you are absorbed in your ego, you leave the state of joy. It is easy, and a very worldly experience, because your ego strokes you, has an insatiable appetite, wants power and more, never has enough, seeks to take advantage of others, is in it only for self-gain, is not inclusive but exclusive, is shallow and on shaky ground, feels that the present good can disappear, is never happy nor feels fulfilled, and will destroy the real you to keep itself alive. That's the low-life experience, and the way most people misunderstand, thinking that is the payoff. It's an experience that moves downward from joy, to ego, to an unfulfilled life.

The high experience is to move from JOY to WISDOM to LOVE! Being in joy is an expression of wisdom. Our favorites:

❋ Richard Branson, who is in a constant state of rip-roaring play, delight, awe, wonder, and excitement—yet he has more than 50,000 employees and does death-defying adventures;

❋ Oprah, who has re-invented herself dozens of times and done so with the whole world watching. She maintains and exudes a radiant spirit and is on a quest to serve infinitely more and better;

❋ His Holiness The Dalai Lama, dedicated to creating an awareness of life—he has seen his country stolen and 1.2 million Tibetans killed, and yet he still gently smiles and forgives the Chinese government for the pain and torment they have caused. The Dalai Lama smiles, chortles, laughs, and enjoys every encounter with the zest of a young, innocent child and he is seventy-five, as of this writing.

❋ Dr. Muhammad Yunus has blessed one hundred million women to enjoy economic freedom with his creation of micro-credit, and he lives in ever-exuding delight.

Now it is your turn to live in the joy-in-spirit, like Branson, Oprah, His Holiness, Yunus and many others. We give you the assignment to inspire others to be and live fully in the joy-in-spirit!

Wisdom is love-in-action. Wisdom which passeth all understanding is available to each of us, according to all the Holy Scriptures. True wisdom is a constant knowing of your continual connection with your Divine Source, which is Love.

U R here to be in total JOY! Enjoy your Joy!

Mark Victor Hansen and Bill Froehlich

P.S. We believe the reader should be advised as to the state of mind of the authors. We had fun writing this, we were and R in the joy-in-spirit writing for you. We hope you had fun and enlightenment reading it.

This is our invitation and permission to you to realize and manifest your true GREATNESS! And below is a future reward:

YOU ARE INVITED

TO THE RED CARPET WORLD TOUR PREMIER

OF

U R THE SOLUTION

ON

THE

BIG SCREEN

Go

To

www.urthesolutionthebook.com

15

ACKNOWLEDGMENTS

We are both extraordinarily thankful to so many for so much. We have taken insights and wisdom from more than 120 years of sublime experiences, friendships, parents, teachers, scholars, soothsayers, and, yes, even naysayers. If we have forgotten anyone, we take full responsibility for so doing and request your humblest acceptance of our deepest gratitude.

No one thanks God and the Universe for being generous, friendly and supportive of our efforts; we are elated to be alive, sharing our delirious delights in this book—thanks be to God and the Universe.

Our agent, Bill Gladstone, has been a phenomenal supporter, contributor, and encourager since we created the idea for the book together over a fun luncheon during a seminar break. Thanks, Bill, for expanding our world of possibility and seeing that what our time needs is a fable to show hope for those who feel hopeless.

Steve Wilson, president and CEO of Fast Pencil, for believing in our dream and being willing to pull out all the stops to make the impossible, possible. And for demonstrating that a book can be published virtually overnight, and make it into bookstores and club stores almost instantly—thanks to POD (Print on Demand) technology, which is helping change the world and make it an infinitely better place for everyone, now.

John Kilcullen, the marketing maven, who is helping us outreach to more millions than any series other that his *Dummies* books or Mark's *Chicken Soup for the Soul.*

To Rob Johnson, independent graphic designer, who worked tirelessly and almost around the clock to produce a magnificent cover.

Michael Ashley, aka Mash, CTO of Fast Pencil, who brilliantly makes all the e-technology harmonize to realize electronic books for us.

Dan Seward, illustrator par excellence, for hearing our dreams and creating illustrations that invite readers to *see* our story and compel them to keep reading.

Melody Culver, our heaven-sent editor, was a delight to work with. Her sharp eye corrected technical flaws and her intuitive heart provided suggestions that made the book better—and she did it all really fast!

Seana Norvell, for making our publicity happen so seamlessly and perfectly, awakening people to the existence of our book.

Crystal Dwyer, for her love, affection, and complete understanding of what it takes to realize a masterpiece.

John Pitre, artist and inventor extraordinaire, for kindly allowing us to share his phenomenal art with a reading audience that we believe will love him as we do.

To Darby Angel, CEO & Chairman of AngelWorld Entertainment Inc, who sees our desire to make this into a major picture like *Avatar* and is dedicated to realizing it on the big screen and throughout other media as well. Darby says, "Mark and Bill, you two are the most substantive writers in Hollywood, and this message needs to get out there."

We appreciate Tony Calsolaro for his friendship and for introducing Mark to Bill as doppelgangers and celebrity look-a-likes. That helped us befriend one another and ultimately led to this book.

We thank our friend Paul Roper for giving us wisdom, guidance and insight along the way.

For Mark's executive assistant, Debbie Lefever, for handling hundreds of details so he could write without ceasing and for taking the fabulous photo of Mark on the back cover; and Karen Schoenfeld, Mark's controller, for magically keeping everything under control and working effectively.

We thank our friends Jennifer McColm and Cynthia Kersey, for allowing us to share their remarkable stories with the world.

Bill would like to acknowledge some special relationships that made the journey of this book and to this book possible and worthwhile:

Pamela Barlow, for her love, support and special friendship that expands my sense of family; Allan Jay Friedman, for the unbreakable bond of brotherhood through thick and thin; Chris Dickie, for his friendship, trust and offering the words and ideas concerning quantum physics; Ginny Partridge, for steadfast friendship and encouragement; Garner Simmons and Mike Haller, for laughs on the links and the loyalty of friendship; Michele LaFleur, for her prayerful support, shared joy and friendship; Brooks Wachtel, for his enduring friendship, kindness and endless knowledge of films and film history; Peter Giagni and Wayne Alexander, for their help, support and representation in the entertainment business and for being trustworthy; Steve Lafferty, for his guidance, support and friendship throughout the Hollywood hustle & hassle; Steve Glodney and Melody Young, for friendship and financial guidance; Bruce Breslau, for his persistent friendship and good heart; Andy

Orgel, for friendship and the promising projects to come with global media ventures; Brian Wright, for sharing his artistry and for his spiritual mentoring and guidance; and a very special kiss from the heart to Catherine Ruddy, for the journey together and the understanding of happiness it brings to both of us.

We deeply thank all of you and anyone we may have inadvertently forgotten. Lastly and vitally, to our Beloved Reader, a heartfelt expression of gratitude for taking this journey with us!

YOU ARE INVITED
TO THE RED CARPET WORLD TOUR
PREMIER
OF
U R THE SOLUTION
ON
THE
BIG SCREEN
Go
To
www.urthesolutionthebook.com